A Time To Live

A COUNTRY BOY'S LIFE
THROUGHOUT THE 20TH CENTURY

by

C. Gordon Porter

ISBN-13: 978 -1490398860
ISBN-10: 1490398864

*This book is dedicated
to my wonderful family and friends, past and
present, who have always surrounded me
with their love and support.*

*And to my community —
there's no better place or time for
a "country boy" to live.*

C. Gordon Porter

CONTENTS

C. Gordon Porter

C. Gordon Porter

This is a short historical life account of a farmer's son throughout the changing times of the 20th century. It follows his experiences as a young farm boy living a simple life to the more complex times of electronics, educational advancements, and entertainment of his adulthood. The author used his own paintings and photos to help highlight his thoughts and stories.

Pictured in the cover photo: C. Gordon Porter with his great grandnephew, Daniel Meza.

C. Gordon Porter

PREFACE

The first few years of my life weren't much different than how life had been for a couple centuries before. The transition from the horse drawn implements to the horsepower engines was happening in the 1930's. I was old enough, born in 1925, to tell you what I observed.

The country life stayed the same until electricity was being distributed to the farms at this time; many farms were still waiting for the lines to come from the power company. New telephone poles and wires brought the services of both phone and electricity that was welcomed. Looking at the marks on the poles the climbers made to add the crossbars and insulators on top and the rolls of wire still linger in my mind.

Pumping water from the wells was a great time saver. Instead of a few gallons an hour by the hand pump now with the time saving electric pumps for a few cents it could pump hundreds of gallons. A good well was worth the price of the farm, the demand was so important raising the livestock. Spraying the fruit trees with the water and spray materials on our farm added income that was produce to buy the first refrigerators to replace the iceboxes few had. The electric stove and hot water heaters replaced the wood and coal stoves. Chopping piles of wood with an ax back then was a must.

The first radios in 1932 had large magnet speakers so everyone in the room could hear without using the headphones. Not just for the one at a time to listen had become a new source of entertainment, we all could turn the dial and hear about the selected programs or the news around the world with three or four limited broadcast stations. Before this, the news came from the party line crank phones or by mail delivered by the stagecoaches then the railroad express. A little later the movie theaters had newsreels.

The automobile was making its progress by going from a front hand crank I learned on, to an electric starter. Many of these improvements led to the paving of dirt and gravel to stone and tar roads. One of the big advantages was we could visit our local cousins and be there in minutes for an invited meal and then drive back home in time to do the evening chores. When the old worn out autos were replaced, we fitted the chassis with a wagon box, and made a "new" rubber tire wagon. This lead to a rubber balloon tired tractor to pull it. Soon the horse drawn equipment was obsolete, meaning the horses were no longer needed. Gasoline was so cheap at that time (the low price of twenty-nine cents a gallon) it became a great saving not to have to fill the big barn full to the rafters for animal's winter supply.

More acres could be added to the farmer's workload and efficiency was greatly increased for more production. The small acreage inefficient farms were sold to the larger ones and that ended many small farm businesses, most of our own farmland ended up being sold. It is getting to be a much greater demand for food production to feed the growing world population, with empty stomachs becomes a demanding hazard.

As you read these memoirs you will begin to see the transitions that I have witnessed. It is really just starting a whole different way of living from the developing years. The powerful resources and new laws of change had begun ... and I was a part of it all.

CHAPTER 1
The Farm Biblical View

The physical work establishing a typical farm on virgin soil for the purpose of owning a farm business to support a family was very demanding. I will try to make this as accurate as what I can remember and with the help of notes found in the original homestead. I saw many important changes that might be causing our present environmental concern. I used "biblical" in the heading because there were some so-called plagues similar to the time of the Exodus.

In 1950 we had an invasion of army worms that were about to devastate the wheat crop just before harvest. Fortunately, the centralized school in Barker offered an aeronautical course and had a landing strip. John Denton, a discharged World War II air force pilot, owned an aircraft biplane used for dusting crops, it was used to help control these worms. These pests covered the roads making the roads slippery for my new 1950 automobile. I also have observed the battle against Gypsy moths and the fungus Dutch Elm disease infestation we saw the that has destroyed most of our graceful Elm shade trees. They grew along the beautiful hedgerows and made a good place for the pheasants to have their nests. It provided good hunting during the open season, the pheasants made a good meal and the dog proved he could hunt.

In the last few years, I've noticed the sudden absence of toads, frogs and honeybees; a change that seemed quite alarming. Diesel fuel could be partly a cause with the skies full of traveling jets burning millions of gallons per day, large semi-trucks and farm equipment with their exhausts. Also the frequent use of pesticides could be helping the problem, and yes, even my riding lawn tractor adds more pollution. (These fumes could have an effect on our health and weather conditions I believe).

In contrast, in the 1930's my brother Art and I would spend

all day Saturday taking turns mowing the homestead and tenant house lawns so they would look good for Sunday. All the mowing was done with a hand pushed reel type lawnmower using no fuel except a glass of raw milk, and mother's homemade yeast bread or rolls spread with homemade butter that was separated from the buttermilk with a large wooden spoon and bowl for our muscle fuel.

CHAPTER 2
The Farm Homestead

The land for the homestead was surveyed and purchased in 1824 by my ancestors from the Holland Land Company, Batavia, New York. It was covered with virgin trees that grew there after the 10,000-20,000 year glacier period. At that time it was a lakebed that extended to a higher ridge from Lake Ontario about eight miles. During the Glacier age I guess with all the ice melting made the lake much larger leaving many small rounded stones that had washed up to build the cobblestone houses along the ridge. The location of this farm was two miles south of the lake at the present time 2010. I don't have any records to know when the lake receded to its present location.

As a young boy I was always fascinated to find sandstone rocks that were left by the glacier. We carried them to the rock piles at the end of the field and taking one of the sandstones by giving it a hard blow with a hard granite rock I could open them seeing seashell forms and fern fossils knowing at some time the weather conditions must have been almost a tropical temperature to be locked inside from maybe millions of years ago. These still can be found in this region where the sandstones were deposited; it's enough to arouse your imagination.

My great, great grandfather William B. Fox cleared the farmland after he purchased it in 1824; then the real physical work began. He was just married the year before they came and had their first of twelve children. Surely his expanding family put pressure on him to survive. Building the homestead, the barn, and out buildings were a real project using only the raw materials that were on the land. It must have taken him a few strenuous years to accomplish. Eventually both his older sons were old enough to be of help but they left to be Civil War soldiers in 1861. The development of the community began after the land was established and was now able to support them enough to raise their families on property they owned. In many cases, this was typical of neighbors helping neighbors by trading their labor back and forth. With additional hands, manpower was added for certain harvesting procedures that required more oxen and horses working to speed up the harvest before the season changes. About one hundred years later I can remember in my time this was still happening while chopping the field corn stalks to fill each close neighbor farmer's new silo with corn silage.

When the silos were full, the weight of the silage squeezed some of the juices out for the fermentation to begin its preservation process ... a means to keep the food from getting moldy. The gases given off were deadly for a short time, so when I climbed up to open the top door to fork down an evening supply for the cows, the air at the top had to be clear. This took about two weeks. I remember seeing small clumps of moldy silage along the edge that was discarded from being used as fodder. A few bushel baskets were filled full with its alcohol smell and we gave each cow her allowed amount. It was top dressed with some appealing ground grain sometimes mixed with a little molasses that the cows liked to make a good daily milk supply. This yearly task when finished. gave a comfortable relief of supply as winter approached of knowing the animals would have plenty to be fed until the spring renewal cycle began in a few weeks planting corn after Easter Sunday.

In the first few years the farmers and their families gathered mostly on a Sunday afternoon for a picnic. Being together, they discussed community affairs for its needs to make it something else besides the regular daily routines. With the local farms now established it became a cooperative friendship with committees forming the new ideas. They voted a chairman and with its present members discussed what the outside world had to offer to satisfy their minds of living a good life along with keeping them in the community. Some had the urge to take their families homesteading to the Midwest, western prairies and beyond, and did leave for what they thought would be greater opportunities in the west.

Building the log cabin school the children were first taught reading, writing and arithmetic with only limited books. Churches formed locally around 1824. It wasn't long before a new building plan was on their minds and as the spinning wheels turned out the wool threads the women talked their heads off about what 'could be.' Soon, with the craftsmanship of the carpenters, County Line Corners had a new church and a schoolhouse for the teaching and worshiping their children so needed.

With the school built for the education of the children, the women started to talk about their right to vote. This topic was well discussed and often argued. In a letter written by my great grandmother, she said,

The question now arises "what is a woman's mission", this question can be answered in various ways. It is not entirely in supplying the physical wants of her family, she is created for a higher and more noble purpose than this, and holds the responsible position in life, even more so than that of man; her capability for doing good is far greater than she, herself realizes. It is not necessary that she should enter the field of public life, in order to accomplish her purpose; her mission should begin in her own home; this should be made the dearest and happiest spot on earth, where the wife and mother should find her purest, deepest pleasures...Nor is this all of the woman's mission, under whatever circumstances she may be placed she should use both her influence and example for the overthrow of wrong and the establishment of right, as Gov. Cornell has just signed the Bill authorizing woman to vote for school officers of all grades, she should use her power to save children ...

Tamar M. Porter, circa 1880

The stagecoach route provided limited passengers with a mail delivery to the post office. Somehow before the railroad came to Millers in 1876 it had to make the connection with the main railroad line that went through the center of the county. A grocery store with supplies was opened for business. All were excited about this new addition because it was a place to go locally for the necessities.

Most everyone started to get acquainted with marriages and funerals and by the ending of the dreadful Civil War the memories of the past were being told by the original settlers and the country was on the move. Mechanical inventions began to spring up and with the mobility meant no turning back. The progress they experienced could almost be compared with what I saw in the Twentieth Century.

The metal candle mold they used was still saved and resting on the beam shelf upstairs in the homestead. Candlelight was used sparingly mostly to aid light to the bedrooms checking to see all were tucked in and comfortable and for checking the fireplace and the stoves for safety reasons.

My great, great grandfather cleared the land by using the ax, saw, scythe and oxen as the power to pull out the stumps. I can remember the yokes that were hung up in the barn for years that were used around the necks of the oxen for hauling and small yokes hand carved out of lightweight basswood that fit on a person's shoulders and partially around the neck. A century later, I still used the yoke to carry pails of water to the chickens being raised in the brooder houses. Most everything was handmade with a few exceptions. Hardwood was used for making furniture, cabinets, trim and flooring and what was left over made excellent fuel for cooking and heating. The hemlock pinewood weathered better and was used mostly for siding the sheds and out buildings. Oxen were gone and horses were the power when I was young.

To build the homestead, a hand auger for making holes to wooden pin the beams and frames together for the barn and house were used. Also used were handmade wooden planes with tempered steel metal blades. These blades forged hot when the colors for hardness were favorable and then were cooled in water. They were wedged onto the handmade wooden planes and used for shaving the wood for a minimum clearance of doors, windows and anything else, to fit smoothly. Square iron handmade nails are still found in the old house sidings. Most everything else from the homestead was sold at the auction. The spinning wheels, washtubs, furniture, vinegar barrels, milking equipment, etc. are gone but not forgotten. While they might have lost their useful identity they remain very clear in my memory.

Gardening tools, barrel hoops and staves, with a crank attached to a three-foot diameter sandstone wheel that ran through a pan of water underneath, always used to keep razor sharp most anything that needed sharpening. I remember turning the crank for my father sharpening the mowing machine blades for cutting hay. A clevis was hooked to the hay rope tied with a bowline knot in back of the horses for pulling the hay up to the above mows. This hay rope knot was a favorite one for the Boy Scouts to learn to tie, and was used for its ease and non-slipping abilities. Homemade hinges and cast-iron door locks are still on the homestead doors today.

Blocks and tackles were used for hoisting up a butchered hog to dress it out. Wire loops were used for catching the big mean old rooster for a delicious Sunday dinner. A hand cranked chain pump was used to bring up the hard fresh spring water from the well and was located just outside the dining room in front of the dining room door of the house as I can remember. This well was no longer used because electricity became available and a pure good fresh water well that was located a few hundred feet south west of the house piped to the large tank made it easy to pump lots of good clean drinking water for the house and barn. The lime in the water was always a cleaning problem from the lime build-up in the teakettle. Maybe the lime that filtered through the shale rock below was good for living long lives, my mother drank it most all her adult farm life, she lived almost to be 102 years old. We used dehydrated lime sparingly around the areas in back of the tied animals for sanitation and freshness.

The Homestead

The Homestead Tennant House

Tenant house was located across the driveway from the main home and is where I was born and where we lived for much of my younger years. The house had no plumbing which made life of a city gal, my mother, a challenge. While adjusting to lesser conditions, happiness was building and the outlook was always promising.

For my father and mother in the 1930's, the depression years were tough. While money was scarce, eating a bag of butter and salted popcorn that each cost twenty-five cents from Bye's Popcorn Stand in Olcott, NY was topnotch. Something as small and simple as a bag of popcorn chased away the worries occasionally.

Cistern water was used for washing, but rain water was softer and always made better suds used for baths and washing clothes. I was with my father when he would kneel down to the rain water catch basin, located below the freeze line, and pailed up a few of pails to use. I remember that he carried a pocket watch in his bib overalls saw it fall into the water going to the bottom. He never swore but on rarest of occasions would say, "Judas Priest!" I suspect he wasn't the first to lose his watch and guess there are probably more watches down there. From then on, he tied a shoestring on his shoulder strap and connected it to the watch.

The dishes were rinsed by the boiling steaming always-hot teakettle drinking water. Farm people were very careful to sterilize the best they could everything to guard against the bacteria pertaining to edible contact. Very seldom a doctor was needed except for contagious diseases or a dismembered finger.

Much of the water was used to spray the fruit trees, and the handy old spray rig would put out fires that could have been disastrous. Our rig occasionally helped save the neighbors barn from grass fire. Using plenty of water kept the spring flowing from becoming stagnant, no purifying chemicals were used; it was a pure deep ground filtered liquid, hard to duplicate anything better.

CHAPTER 3
The Early Life

My first memory of concern at age four was the 1929 depression when Herbert Hoover was President. The word came that the banks were closing at noon. I never forgot how upset my Grandpa Orson became. I was within hearing range when he told my father to go to the Lyndonville bank and draw out the savings, which he did. At noon the bank closed and locked its doors, many missed the deadline losing their entire savings. When their mortgages came due, some farmers had no money to pay, filed bankruptcy and were told to leave. Their farms were sold to ones that had cash and lost to them forever. Money was scarce but those who met the deadline were able to take advantage of the bargains.

The trend of the small farms like ours has practically disappeared by selling a good share of their land to the larger farms. In New York State or in the USA as you read this account, can see the reason why? In order to survive the new equipment we purchased advanced our production very rapidly; then instead of one hundred chickens we could handle four hundred selling the eggs to the hatchery. We installed water fountains in each pen eliminating carrying pails of water, a real labor saver. Trucks, rubber tire tractors and grain combines are a few examples of how farming was changing. At the present time some of the large tractors are guided by sky satellite in making better use of the land with straight rows in the cornfields. These new hand-held cell phones; what a help they are in case of a break down. One man can run a machine that eliminates many workers with the harvesting.

By having my father buy a milking machine that could milk all four quarters at once meant I could milk the five cows alone very easily while he could be doing something else. Before, when he couldn't help with the milking the five cows it was a real chore for me alone. Many times he did the milking while I had school music and sports activities. We didn't have enough money or land to expand. Today the few dairy farmers that sold milk to the neighbors are gone. The much larger herds have made this a commercial enterprise some shipping a loaded semi-trailer full of milk to be pasteurized. This has happened in almost every farm product producing businesses; this really changed the rural way of life with the larger farm operations working more efficiently. Our church was full of farm families, now very few are left in the congregation that can be counted.

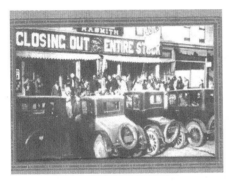

Main Street
Barker, New York

1929
Homestead Tennant House

Standing in front of the homestead, Burton wore great grandfather Simeon's hat and cane in 1973, to celebrate the 1813 Town of Somerset Anniversary.

I was born in the tenant house on the homestead property. Our house had no plumbing or drinking water till about 1932. Later a fresh well water line was dug and connected to the barn line which had running spring water electrically pumped from the well. Second in line to get water was the barn and then the tenant house. Each morning Dad carried a pail of drinking water from the barn to our house for drinking and cooking.

Burton (my dad) and Ruth (my mother), with sons Arthur and Gordon (me), moved into the Homestead after Orson's death in 1937. This move changed things for my family. Every room in the homestead was much larger. The living room was adequate to have choir rehearsal practices weekly and committee meetings that involved many community affairs to discuss.

CHAPTER 4
Farm Water and Electric System

The main first electric power line between Lyndonville and Barker came through our property 1568 County Line Road in the Town of Somerset, Barker, NY in the 1920's and into our homestead where my grandfather lived. A large transformer was placed near us giving us electric power before our neighbors. A 1000-gallon storage tank was placed in the cellar. I still don't know how grandpa managed to have the heavy, large steel tank put down in the cellar, but he figured it out somehow. He had an electric water pump installed for filling it with cold spring water from the good well about 300 feet south west of the house and maintaining thirty pounds pressure with a gauge attached piped the water for the bathroom, kitchen and the livestock barn. A large upright tank next to the wood cooking stove had the water flow into a cast iron unit in the firebox where water was self-circulated through it providing plenty of hot water; this was a new welcomed improvement for a rural community. Also added was a bathtub and a flushing toilet that emptied into a homemade septic tank with a

 maple plank baffle separating the waste to be digested by bacteria. The liquid run off went down the clay tiled drain to a small ditch and most of it evaporated because of the small amount of water used back then. The rest did eventually end up in a larger run-off ditch where the abundance of wild peppermint grew; I sampled the leaves for its flavor that was used in the peppermint chewing gum packaged sticks sold at the local grocery store. I helped clean the septic tank a couple of times. We didn't have these improvements for our tenant house for years, only an

outhouse toilet. All drainage was downstream far from the good well. There were five dug wells on the farm and two were used. The neighbor (Tripps) used the south well beyond the end of the Yates Center road.

I can remember Carrie Tripp, a stunning woman not a hair out of place, because visiting in the neighborhood was common. Once when she visited Grandpa and Grandma Porter I walked in front of her while she was talking and Grandpa said to me "Gordon, say 'excuse me,'" my first lesson of being polite. The neighbors visiting back and forth were about the only way to communicate any news in the neighborhood and to exchange the local gossip. I have found many cancelled stamped envelopes knowing they did write to each other about the exciting news of the day so they did mail letters through the post office to each other frequently as well. Soon they had local correspondents from different communities writing for the newspaper.

Our tenant house had a small amount of electricity, which was a light fixture in each room and floor receptacles, but no electric appliances. We had wood stoves that also burned coal, a coal bin that held two or three tons for winter in the cellar used to burn all night to keep the house warm. Around 1928 I can just remember a pair of head speakers connected to the crystal radio with an aerial that went from the house to the barn. It wasn't very good reception but it was more than some had. It's possible that my uncle Howard, being familiar with early electronics, may have set this up for our family.

My mother's brother Uncle Howard Bloomfield was a radio engineer who helped build the equipment for broadcasting and was one of the first announcers and hosts for live programs for WHAM or WHEC Rochester at that time. He had an organist living at his house at Arnette Blvd, Rochester who added music to the broadcast.

We soon had an upright tube radio that was just introduced to the public in about 1932. On Sunday mornings before going to church we always listened to the Mormon Tabernacle Choir from Utah. It was such good inspirational Christian music; it seemed to put us into a day of rest from the regular routines of the daily work.

Taking a bath on Saturday night only was done in a round large clothing washbasin with about two inches of warm rainwater, heated on the stove. I'm not sure, but I think my brother Arthur always took his bath first so I had to use the same water with a little added hot rainwater. In the winter we stood on a stool when we got out because it was warmer up higher in the kitchen and mother would dry us with a clean towel. A curtain was hung in the doorway between the kitchen and dining room. Then we would go upstairs to bed. The wastewater was dumped into the sink that had a lead drain pipe that curved through a hole emptying outside into a clay tile drain to a covered catch basin, then to a drainage ditch.

The stovepipe from the living room stove came up through our bedroom and gave off a little heat but the wool blankets were what really kept us warm. As it was often the case, my brother and I slept together. The commode was under the bed and had a cover on it. We had to empty it every morning outside in the toilet (outhouse). On particularly cold mornings we would make a dash for it. This was the way it was with my parent's marriage living 1921 through 1937; no flushing toilet in the house until 1947. A cistern under the kitchen that was filled with rainwater was hand pumped to the sink. It was the only appliance in the house and was used for everything but cooking and drinking, and used sparingly depending on the rains.

Mother would carry the family laundry over to the other house to wash; I remember the scrub board and the bar of homemade lye soap. I helped turned the crank of the wringer with two rollers after the clothes were washed. All that was washed were hung on the clothesline to dry and on the real cold mornings it froze the damp washings to rock solid. As soon as the sun hit them they thawed and became dry and they had that welcoming clean fresh smell again. Grandma Rose made lye soap with butchered pork fat and wood ashes many times on the wood stove when it set she cut into square bars. I can still remember seeing the large cookie tin she used to mold the soap and make a good supply to last quite a while.

CHAPTER 5
Electricity

Early in my life I soon learned the importance of how things were changing from what we were accustomed to the newer, more convenient ways. Even doing the task of hand pumping water for the livestock changed our lives. We pumped only a few hundred gallons a day. I would estimate and our farm was similar to our neighbors with the usual livestock, a team of horses, half a dozen cows milked by hand, pigs, chickens plus the young replacements and maybe a few other animals to carry pails of water to every day of the year.

Fortunately our farm was located between the two villages of Lyndonville and Barker so the power lines were installed making electricity available on our property with a transformer. Both villages had cold storages that required large electric compressors for lowering the individual rooms at a temperature to forty-two degrees, the ideal degree for storing fruit. While there at the cold storage one day, my father asked the floor manager if he would show me the compressor section to see the cooling equipment working. I can still remember the strong smell of ammonia.

The purpose of the cold storages was when the fresh market would be overloaded with fruit, the cold storage would keep it fresh until more profitable prices were reached. Sometimes this didn't happen so the taxes had to be put on hold hoping for a better year.

The storages also had a cold room where they froze ice in one hundred pound sections and handled with grappling hooks could be sold to those who had iceboxes. The ice was used in the warmer days for keeping the milk from souring. We didn't have an icebox, the reason was every penny was accounted for and there was no room in the budget for this luxury. Living on a farm, we had a daily food supply with the added canned fruits and vegetables on the farm so were able to do without quite well.

Fred Thiel's farm bordering the lakeshore in our township near the lighthouse had a side business in the summer of netting the fish in Lake Ontario. He set his nets about two miles out due north of the lighthouse. The fish netted were Blue Pike a freshwater fish. He gutted them, loaded his delivery truck platform, covered the fresh fish with the purchased ice from the Cold Storage, and went door-to-door selling his catch until were all sold.

My father would take a knife and scrape the scales off and fillet them. I remember eating the delicious fish mother cooked in Crisco sort of like lard. In the early 1950's my father and mother took my family to Krepenneck's Restaurant on some Fridays evenings for a blue pike fish fry. It was the best, a real treat from the regular farm food. It's sad to experience the extinction of the blue pike in the Great Lakes. The Iceland Ocean Haddock now is my favorite fish fry.

Very soon my grandfather saw the advantage of these power lines. He had the two homes and barns wired using the electricity. The barn and outside buildings had the wires covered with steel piping to prevent the rodents from gnawing them and possibly causing a fire by the short-circuiting. This convenience made a great change in the way the farm operated comparing to our neighbors and the first appliance available was the electric twenty-five-cycle pump that gave the homestead a flushing towel and bathtub a first in our community. We were without this convenience for my first few adolescent years at our house. A few years later we dug a pipeline to the tenant house from the barn and we then had running fresh drinking well water under pressure from a faucet by the sink.

For a few years the neighbors who lived only a short distance from the lines didn't have electricity and used oil and white gas mantel lamps. They envied our location having this new progressive service from the Niagara Mohawk Power Company. With this service the waterlines to the farm buildings hydrants with shutoff valves were installed to fill the water tubs by just turning the four-knob handle and in no time I could water the livestock eliminating carrying of pails of water and soon installed drinking cups in the cow stable.

Lightning would strike the transformer during a storm and once in a while a violent storm would cut the service a couple of days. This prompted me, being the water boy, to go to the neighbors and hand pump enough water for a couple of days, the remembrance still lingers having the blisters from hand pumping.

Many fall nights with the lights on were spent in the barn packing apples to send to market. I had to stamp each basket cover in black ink through a certified brass stencil with our name and address, apple size U.S.No.1, 2 ½ in. and variety. We always put up quality fruit and what was discarded went to the pigs, hardly anything was wasted. Some years it would rain during the whole blossom season and the bees couldn't do their pollinating and result in a very light crop. We depended so much on the weather and everything while working on the farm, so a loss like this was always felt. When it came to planting and harvesting, the time was limited. All the winter food supply for the family had to be done just at the right time for canning. My mother would stir in a little sugar each day to sweeten the vinegar for the gherkin pickles stored in a large crock. This process would make the pickles taste just right and add so much to the meat and potato dinners once in a while.

CHAPTER 6
Getting the Mail and Trains

Our mail had to be picked up at Millers, a small hamlet one half mile south of the farm. My grandfather would let me ride with him in the 1929 Chevy to get the mail and would give me a penny to buy some licorice or a package of mixed colored candy wafers at the covered candy case. Whenever he got in the car I was ready to jump in, but when he had other business to attend to, he was very firm to say, "not this time."

The mail was delivered by the steam engine trains to the depot at Millers and taken over to the post office at Venesse's store. I can remember helping my father dig the hole for a post to put up a mailbox when rural free delivery started delivering mail from the Post Office in Barker.

Passenger trains were eliminated by my time because of the auto industries advancement for traveling. There were two or three trains a day at the Millers, N.Y. Station. I painted this scene from a black and white photo I had of the original station.

In the spring two carloads of young sheep would be unloaded

and driven down our dirt road by dogs to the Todkill farms north where they would graze all summer. The wool would be sheared and then sent they would travel back in the railroad cars to be used for meat. The Todkills owned the Barker Cold Storage where we sometimes stored our apples.

In the fall, the Hobos would ride on top of the railroad cars. Some would get off at Millers and go over to the old sycamore tree in back of the Depot and camp for the night. Very often they came to the farms during the fruit harvest season and picked our fruit. When we needed apple pickers they were available and ready to start off to be fed by my mother's good free meal. They not only would enjoy the meal, but the smell of good cooking brought many back to the farm each year. They were given cash paid by the bushel they had picked. Sometimes they would stay the night in the empty brooder houses. These small houses been cleaned using the spray rig and were white washed with lime mixed with a strong lye disinfectant and provided a room with a cot and a kerosene heater for their privacy and comfort. A washbasin was available for them to wash themselves each day. Although many had no homes, they weren't bad men. During the depression, jobs were hard to find and free transportation riding on top of the railroad cars brought them close to a place where they could find work and food for a living.

A few were beggars that came to the door to ask for food. They were given some kind of a sandwich made of a homemade bread that satisfied their hunger and then they would leave to go off to who knows where. Most of them were alcoholics that hardly ever sobered up. When they came looking for work they were on a hangover and had to be refused a dependable working job in such a controlled state of health. It was sad to see a human being suffer this kind of life. I never forgot this and think the world would be better if there was some way to kick the habit instead of leading to disasters we hear about that could have been avoided. A time to live a happier life is there for us, but it is up to us to make the choice.

CHAPTER 7
Academies, the First Rural Schools

According to my mother Ruth Beatrice (Bloomfield) Porter a former and first Town of Somerset Historian, Irving Hotaling, surgeon in the Civil War, came to Somerset and purchased in 1878 the old Methodist church, moved it across the street and established the "SOMERSET ACADEMY." The building was divided with folding doors so the front part could be used as a public hall and the back room for school purposes. There also was a room upstairs which provided another classroom. The curriculum covered the 8th, 9th and 10th grades. Public-spirited citizens served an oyster supper and raised money to purchase the needed books an encyclopedia and *Webster's Unabridged Dictionary*.

While I was working on our local family history, I found that my great grandfather Simeon Porter had been born 1837 in Michigan. When he was one year old his father died in 1838. His mother, a widow, was unable with seven children to support them there and had to leave Michigan and travel back to New York State to live with her parents. Not long after the family arrived in New York, she soon passed away too. Simeon was unfortunate to lose his parents so young. He was sent away to a relative far away only to return to his distant relative Aunt Pennsylvania Barker, David Barker's wife who sheltered him. In his pencil notes he mentioned he got his education by joining the Fraternity in Somerset where members taught him to learn how to read and write.

As I was reading *The Story of Somerset,* a small book written by my mother, I began to think about the education of my grandfather Orson Barker Porter born in October 28, 1868. I found there were a local log cabin church and school built in 1826 located on the Lum farm near the County Line Corners, Niagara side about one half mile north of my homestead. It was walking distance and around 1874 he probably attended the first six or seven grades. At that time was a diary note dated on Jan. 22, 1880 "the teacher is having trouble with some unruly boys and has left."

I read that Orson's age was maybe eleven or twelve and suspect that he might have been one of the 'unruly' ones. Who knows? There must have been a local log cabin school near the county line corners. This was before he enrolled to further his education with the Academy Institution of Advanced Learning five miles away at Yates Center.

I found a small stamped envelope in the saved records that had the opening and closings dates of the Academies across New York State where Orson attended the local Yates Academy. I found a little booklet with the pages full of classmate's signatures  including some names of other local familiar to me of family names that attended the academy. I have enjoyed reading these saved articles and pencil notes that for years laid to rest in the bottom drawer of the old homestead. There is a sign "YATES CENTRE ACADEMY" north of Lyndonville, NY located on Route 63. He lived five miles almost directly west at the Porter Fox Homestead on the Niagara side of the County Line; very fortunately he received his schooling from this Academy. The student friends wrote little clever notes wishing him good luck and included the dates from January 2, 1883 through March 17, 1887 giving him the 8th through 10th grade education making his age around fifteen through eighteen. The penmanship and intelligent scripts were exceptional from the group of these very well educated classmates at that time.

My father attended first eight grades in the fairly new school Yates #7 at County Line Corners, then to the Lyndonville High School. To follow the trend, I attended Yates #7 through the fifth grade before transferring to Barker High School.

About 1937 Ralph Weeks began a bus service called the Ridge Road Express at Jeddo, and started busing students from a large area to the Barker High School, built in 1911 of all twelve grades. I started riding the new bus route to the school in 1937 and fortunately took private lessons from the band director Charles Barone. He came to our house with a new trumpet my folks bought for $50. Every week Mr. Barone taught me how to play and read treble clef music for an hour lesson of $1.00. What an opportunity!

It's funny how different things come to light living at the homestead. There was a cornet in a much worn leather case never touched in the attic I could have used myself. Reading the Civil War letters of my great uncle to my great grandmother mentioned practicing in the battlefields before going on picket. I'm sure the practicing could have been with the company band playing his cornet but this is only a hunch.

With a little practicing I entered the school band playing the third part in the trumpet, cornet section. Being small in numbers and not having enough high school band students he increased the numbers using the lower grades for substitution to balance the right amount of instruments to make up a competitive band that included myself.

I rode the bus to the Band State Competition held in Albany. It was an old used Greyhound Bus that Mr. Weeks owned with spare tires fastened in the rear and air cushion seats. Our director Mr. Barone gave us instructions to raise our instruments together when he raised his baton for us to play. He made sure we were tuned up with a B-flat carefully checking each of us with his perfect-pitched ear to sound and play our best and we did without a fancy uniform like most bands had, we all wore white shirts and black pants. We tied first place competing with the entire selected top performing high school bands across the State. When we played "The Stars and Stripes Forever" little very young Beebe a grade school student played her Piccolo part flawlessly. She had a very musical talented mother I'm sure influenced her practicing to perfection. The judges were pleased how well we performed, so all the practicing preparing for this event became a thrill of my lifetime.

CHAPTER 8
First Field Trip

I went to the County Line Corners Country School in the 1930's from age five to age ten. This school was built in the 1890's. There is a photo of the classes when my father attended about 1910. I remember my grandfather Orson Porter, Harry Pratt and Dur Kenyon were the trustees that hired the schoolteachers who taught my father and then me. I can still remember Dur sitting on the bench smoking his cigar at the country store joking with another friend and as I went into the store hearing his hilarious silly laughter. Don't get me wrong he was a smart old guy and knew how to make a comfortable living, but he seemed to really enjoy his life.

Now a repair garage, it was the Yates #7 school that had two-rooms the first four grades in one room and in the other room had fifth through eighth. There was no plumbing, just outhouses and a full pail of spring water with one dipper for all to use for a drink. I remember someone visiting the school that brought "Life Boy Soap" samples so we could wash our face and hands better. There were a few very poor students that came to school without washing so this was a real welcomed treat, and I couldn't wait to get home to show my folks. We had white ivory soap at home for our baths, hands and face; I remember using a bar of soap for carving a miniature statue of a dog. With very few toys, this was an added plaything. Mother had a box of soap flakes for washing the dishes; Grandmother Rose made lye soap on the wood stove for washing the weekly clothes on Mondays.

Grandpa Orson, being a school trustee, decided with only three of us in my class in the fourth grade at the country school to take us on a field trip to Lockport to see the textile industries. Cotton was beginning to be the wonder fabric so he took us to the one that was on the south side of the canal just west of the widest bridge in the world at that time. You can see what is left of the concrete flooring from the bridge today.

I remember the cotton cloth they were manufacturing had floral designs. I suppose it would be made into shirts, aprons or dresses. As it came off the rollers it was put on bolts to be delivered. We saw the whole process from the beginning to the end; it was a great experience to be able to see what others did for a living other than farming.

My birthday is just after the fourth of July celebration and most every year the company of relatives visited to taste the ripe sweet Bing cherries. I remember very distinctly getting a one-piece wool bathing suit that was held by its shoulder straps for my birthday. I put it on but quickly discovered that it prickled so much I told my folks I couldn't stand to wear it for even a minute. I ended up wearing just my shorts for swimming at the lake.

On the way back from the textile industry we stopped at the Kenan, Randleigh Registered Jersey Farms to watch through a round window from the ice cream parlor the cows being milked by vacuum milking machines. This was very advanced technology newly developed in the middle 1930'S maybe a decade before other dairy farms in the locality had a chance to use the new method. In the Ice Cream Parlor, Grandpa treated us with an ice cream cone While I can't be sure, it may have been my first ice cream in a cone. It was an experience that made me stop in for their milkshakes whenever I had the chance.

Studying about the cotton plants being grown in the southern states, the imported slaves were the human harvesting machines before the cotton picking harvest machinery was invented to replace them. Many were treated unholy as humans only a few decades before I was born. Slavery and Wars, unless you were personally involved, there is no way I can make a comment to satisfy those human sacrifices that disrupted the love that was given at the first breath of innocence. We sang some of their rhythm spiritual songs in the country school I truly believed it gave me the innocence of humanity.

Having a paddlewheel ride on the Mississippi a few years ago with one of my children and family, we saw the barges loaded with bales of cotton being taken up stream. Back then the bales were unloaded to the railroads; some could have been transported to Lockport, N. Y. I assumed. Today most of my clothes in the closet are no longer made in the USA. This has had a major impact here. Many of the local industries have closed down or moved out of the state or elsewhere. To compete with the foreign manufacturers we can grow the cotton but must figure a way to bring back the essential industries. It will come back; time has a way to straighten things out if given a chance.

My memories keep coming back thinking what I did many times as an adolescent. For one thing just alone sitting under the hickory nut tree to be company for my father while he was plowing the nearby field with old horses Bill and Fritz, coming back after a round or two to stop giving the team and himself a rest in the shade, he would take the old clay jug remove the corn cob cork for a sip of cool refreshing spring water. I would have a nutmeat I opened for him. The progress of tilling the soil was so slow and hazardous in the rocky glazier laden ground; it seemed forever to plow just a few acres to be ready at wheat planting time. The time must have been late summer in the early 1930's, I liked being near my father.

I would find a few hickory nuts and with a small stone break the hard shell open with another stone used as a hammer. To eat the small nutmeat was such a treat. I also broke open the sandstones to see the fossils imbedded millions of years ago for eternity. I hope old Mrs. Tripp living across the country road wasn't watching out her window to see me cracking stones probably thinking something wrong with me cracking stones together or maybe she had done the same at one time in her early life to understand. Her neighbor Mrs. Davis would come out of her house and yodel like the Swiss with a very strong yodeling voice that carried over to the hickory tree. At times her husband Ray would have just as strong a voice but would use every swear word that Satan gave him. Despite his salty language, we always knew when it came for a needed lift to help as a neighbor, he was always congenial to lend a hand.

There weren't many young people that ever had that opportunity to put their imagination together of how the past was so long ago except reading it in a book. At my age to have it exposed right before me, out where I was not lonely at all, just wondering where everything all began. Just sitting out under a tree in a wooded area maybe hunting or resting on a stump while hiking to catch your breath I can hear the quietness and a sense to meditate. It's so fulfilling to receive that peace I need sometimes of really being close to the Almighty and soon find the comforting peace I was needing. I guess that's why they build the massive Cathedrals for such comfort. We have most everything we need or want but should take a short break to unwind.

My mind sometimes is full of ideas of how we can harness the power of the sun or wind given to us. I would take out the lens from the flashlight and with the sun's ray's burn my name on my baseball bat. There is energy waiting to be used isn't there? We have harnessed the nuclear atom to make electricity but there is the radiation waste we still have to contend with. There are new ideas others have that will answer many of these thoughts, some may come from a dream of reality.

Building a telescope with a lens so powerful and putting it up in space has revealed to us the vastness of uncharted space. Today people still wonder and try to figure precisely how long ago it was not thousands, millions but maybe billions of years ago something happened but there seems to be the more we look there is no end. Does the universes circle around and come back or maybe it does but being such a large expansion with so many galaxies our minds can't comprehend the vast possibilities? I can't help to think what it was before the big bang they claimed how it happened?

Just reading in the newspaper I received today in 2013, I'll quote the scientist, "Our Milky Way is home to at least 17 billion planets that are similar in size to Earth. A new estimate suggests there are more than two Earth-size planets for every person on the globe." Many warm nights in the summer a friend and I slept on the lawn near the homestead with the dog and a cat or two lying by my feet and looking up with no lights on just darkness until your eyes adjust to a view up or way out watching the frequent shooting stars and saw the Milky Way with its lighter streak not knowing or unable to count a small section in the panoramic view. Going camping there may be an opportunity to observe even more of these wonders, when I took my boys up into Canada we slept outside; there was also a spectacular array of northern lights. Living out in the country you are given the freedom to explore your surroundings. We all can't live the same way; the city folks had other advantages that I didn't, but country or city, what a life to live!

We have to leave this up to God that watches over and governs the universe for our existence.

CHAPTER 9
Physical Education

How do you describe education? Knowledge is absorbed into the brain and the "heart" gives us the personality. To be educated you may be an inventor, improviser or in most cases you have to be shown or taught how to do certain things. The trend as I sense it is to change what has been accomplished through the many decades our forefathers gave us through trial and error; the good new ideas take priority if we want to compete with such an open world market today.

When I was young after the age of ten we had no physical exercisers to keep us from putting on weight. It was lifting many sixty pound bushels of apples, potatoes, bags of cabbage, one hundred pound bags of chicken feed or livestock feed to carry into the chicken feed storage area or the animal feed bins in the barn. This was plenty of exercise for building strength. Another part of the job was pumping and carrying gallons of water to the other livestock exerting every muscle in my body giving me an appetite when it came to dinnertime. At night, being exhausted, my blood would rush through my veins and would give me a restful sleep for the next day.

Many of the youths under legal age that came to our farm were so pleased to make a dollar or two so they could buy a candy bar a bottle of glass bottled pop or school clothes for they appreciated every thread. Some off-the-farm friends didn't have this opportunity. This was substituted with sports programs as the schools modernized. The present enforced laws that are made and passed, sort of protected the youths from harming themselves picking a few pounds of cherries, picking up bushels of potatoes or tomatoes or the dropped apples to be sent to the vinegar factory. They still get the exercise with the costly equipment the schools provide probably physically harder than the farm work that was offered back then. The offering was to help lower the cost to harvest the produce for the small business farm owners.

What has happened was the farm owner, like my brother Art who hired these youths, became uneasy about the laws. With the break-even results the orchard ended by hiring the local bulldozer to come and push out the trees. In some cases welfare aid was the substituted income to help the poor families but the training of how the youths could handle the pay for their work now had become absent. This very productive land soon was destroyed of its prime endeavors and the open land has become a labor saving profitable enterprise growing corn, soybeans or hay eliminating the ambitious youths source of income who many now have become overweight. This has kept the lawmakers and the law enforcement busy trying to solve it.

It seemed we were always carrying off heavy stones and at the age of about twelve in 1937 my father taught me how to plow with the steel wheel Fordson tractor. After a few rounds I was on my own out in the seven-acre field trying to plow fairly straight furrows. Once in a while the plow would hit a large stone and it would automatically come unhitched. The stones left in the former lakebed if too large to lift it would be rapped with the heavy log chain we carried and towed to the large rock pile.

While in the fields, I always enjoyed the flights of seagulls that were looking for the unearthed worms and gliding so effortlessly in the wind currents flying fearlessly very close to me. You could tell the time at noon by your shadow being straight north. Where we lived in the flat countryside everything was north and south and east and west, so facing north your shadow would be directly ahead of you and time to go for dinner. On a cloudy day my stomach told with a rumble at eleven assuring my time to stop and go to be fed at dinnertime. Wristwatches weren't used but thought of when we listened to our daily radio episodes offering secret wrist decoders we sent for with cereal box tops. All this physical work gave me a strong appetite and our main meal was at this noontime.

Everything on the farm was an education; the grain had to be just ripe enough to cut and bundled for the sun to dry without sprouting to be thrashed out later, the germ in the wheat was essential for high conception for the pregnancy with the livestock. The hay had to be just at the blossom time to make it taste sweet for the livestock to eat more for higher production. The fruits had to be picked exactly at the right time to make them salable; this was with the poultry and animals for meat too. Timing was so important for harvesting and our strength served its purpose. This land needed to be managed and by giving it the proper care the reward supplied food we all so graciously consume.

CHAPTER 10
Farm Horses and Wagon

The horses were the main source of power. We had to load the big barn full of hay with many loads like this shown. The picture shows Dad (Burton) sitting, Uncle Ken who was visiting with reins, Gordon standing on old Bill, and aunt Helen about the 4th of July.

Being quite tall for my age, it was my job to get the horses ready for their duties by hooking them up for whatever job that had to be done. The first time I had ever done this, I had just turned 12 in 1936. Our team of powerful horses were close friends to me. I fed and groomed them regularly with the curry-comb brushes including their manes and the long tail switches. It must have felt good because when we let them out completely harness free into the pasture the first thing they did was to lie down and roll over I guess scratching their backs, and loosening their muscles, running and racing around the pasture then back to their own places in the barn to be fed their oats haltered and tied. While the stalls were empty, I bed them down with plenty of fresh straw to be ready for a good night rest after a hard day of strenuous work in the field.

When they were in their stalls I had to get them ready for the day's work. I put on their padded collars around their necks for pulling first, then the harnesses of a bunch of leather straps that had to be placed exactly right on their backs, hooking the snaps to the collar at one end and under the tail at the other end, then reaching under hooking the belly strap around the heart girth to keep all in place. I had to put on the bridle opening their mouths and putting in the bit for steering. The reins were snapped on later for control, the bridle in front and back of his ears on top of his head and a strap around his neck and hooked to hold it on. Now with both horses harnessed, I took them to the wagon to hitch up. The four wheel wagon had a tongue made of oak wood about ten feet long was attached to the front axle with the two wheels connected to the tongue. The neck yoke with a center ring was placed crossways and fastened to the collars up front of each horse. In back of them were the whipple (double) trees where two harness straps for each were hooked on for pulling, this made a tight dual connection both front and back on the tongue placed through the yoke ring for pulling, backing up or stopping, or for any of the controlled tasks that the horses performed. The long reins were then put on the wagon for me to drive to the orchard. I was trusted to handle them to take a load of apples to the VB Apple Sauce Canning Factory in Lyndonville where thousands of bushels of apples were dumped in piles to be processed into the famous canned applesauce; it was ten miles round trip keeping on the right side of the road. Each farm I passed I could see what activities were intended for that day. One place had a fruit tree in the front yard that was in blossom at the harvesting time. As I rode by, going and coming back, I wondered why this should out of season ever happen? I had no thought or vision that in a few short years they, the horses and a wooden four wheel wagon, could ever be replaced by a rubber tired tractor that had to be fed a few gallons of fuel to be ready for a day's work.

When we had a load of heavy bundled wheat the command was to back the wagon into the barn, this was quite an upgrade effort for them but they never failed the command. I remember going to the harness shop on Maple Avenue in Lyndonville near the Bank to have the extra pairs of harnesses repaired and fixed to be ready when needed. The breed of horses we owned were called Percheron's a very hardy middle size horse that would pull anything they could move until you said whoa. They would respond to Gee to the right and Haw to the left. They were used for almost everything on the farm. They pulled plows, grain drills, and corn and grain binders. In the 1930's corn binders cut and bundled the corn stalks and were shocked in the fields to dry. The rats made their nests for the free food to feed the young under the shocks and the dog was ready waiting to do his duty when we were loading to take to the barn. Through the winter we would husk a load at a time on the barn floor. We put the ears in the corncrib to dry further, and then to the hand cranked corn sheller later to be ground for chicken, cow and pig feed we then ground up fine for their consumption.

The horse named Max was my favorite, no sharp back bone and just a real friendly animal. When rested up for fun we rode on him through paths in the woods bareback. If I had a friend visit I would hook him up to an old buggy we still had and we'd take a ride. Bill Wolfe the blacksmith made and fitted the spiked horseshoes nailing them to the hoof then bending the nails over. I often thought it might hurt them but I guess it didn't. Wagons all had wooden spoke wheels with smooth medal treads because the roads were dirt or gravel. The farm was divided up into plots of about seven acres. The farm was 87 acres of land and a few acres for the buildings; about half was a variety of fruit trees, crops, grain and hay, most the farms were our size because the machinery was geared to real horsepower.

Beginning as a twelve-year-old boy the experience driving this team for unloading a wagon of loose hay was part of the learning process it takes to be a farmer. It proved how the team of horses gave all the power they had to pull the tons of hay up for winter storage to the second floor of the barn. The load was divided into three sections with slings with metal rings to hook the rope to on the front and back of the load.

Each half sling was made up of two inch by five-foot oak wooden bars fastened together by half-inch ropes spread out across the load. The two halves were locked together in the center of the wagon with a tripping mechanism. The main large rope was fastened to a trolley on a track at the peak of the barn that went from one end to the other end.

There were a series of pulleys at the other end guiding the rope to ground level to where the horses were to do the pulling. As I started the team down a short path I could see every muscle in both of their hind end and legs exerting everything they had to raise the sling full of hay starting to rise up. Their horseshoes were designed with cleats to prevent slippage. As my father would hook on the tripping rope the section went up to the upper open side of the barn to the trolley which would take the hay into a place in the mow tripped by the dangling rope to be forked leveling for the maximum storage. When the towrope would slacken I knew the sling had been tripped and turned the team around to go back after the next sling to unload. After the three sections on the wagon were unloaded into the mow we would go to the field for another load. The outside temperatures near the end of June were hot about ninety-five degrees and even hotter in the loft.

My mother seemed nervous knowing when we were doing this task. She was always needed as a guard to hear any command to stop if something went wrong. There was a dangerous possibility of getting tangled up with the ropes and hollering could save a life. Unfortunately things had happened on other farms, but we survived.

Climbing up high was always a threat and when a storm was brewing. Dad and I had to close the upper open doors quickly hanging on only with one hand and stretching out using a fork to unlock and swing shut and hooks as the wind was picking up. Summer storms have been violent in the open country but through the years we were lucky in my twenty-four years living on the farm the storm damage wasn't a problem.

CHAPTER 11
Depression: Tractors and Ingenuity

When the banks failed in 1929 my father rushed to the Lyndonville bank and withdrew his savings, those years were I called "the lean years," very little spending money.

Many suppers consisted of homemade bread and milk. I don't know what the non-farmers ate, but I bet not much. We had lots of farm animals so we ate pretty good most years.

The rooster that was the bossiest most always ended up for Sunday dinner. He would attack you with his long spurs if you turned your back to him and you knew if you didn't avoid him he would draw your blood. I used a long stiff wire hook to catch him with; it worked great. If the timing was right, off to the chopping block and boiling water was his next and last time for him to be around. Working with animals on the farm some males have this aggressiveness for protecting his flock, it was always wise to watch out for the gander.

We sold hatching eggs to the hatchery and the Rhode Island Red hens were crossed with the Barred Rock roosters to produce baby chicks that would grow larger and bigger for others to raise and sell. The farms are always expanding buy up land to increase the income. We built more chicken coops to double our capacity just like the vegetable and dairy farmers do today. They no longer had five cows but five hundred to a thousand or more. Uncle E.J. Thiel who married my father's sister, owned the hatchery and along with his hatchery he raised thousands of Pekin ducks, once a week he would take a truck load to Cleveland. They were watered and fed along Golden Hill Creek; a small dam at the creek was made for that purpose. This was located near the Thirty Mile Point Light House. My dad rode once with him to Cleveland, and on the way home bought me my first bicycle. I was so excited, now I could ride to school like the rest of the kids.

In 1939 we bought our first rubber-tired tractor a John Deere. The old Fordson tractor had steel wheels that were very noisy, probably partly to blame for the constant ringing in my right ear but I was always eager to drive it. It could plow but was a pain on the sand knolls. If you didn't release the McAdam disk harrow from working the sand knoll the tractor with its steel wheels would dig into the sand and sit there until the team of horses could pull the tractor out. McAdam's had a farm equipment manufacturing business in the Village of Barker; I went there and saw the McAdams casting the bearings. They had formed sand molds then they poured the hot metal into the sand shapes. Small businesses flourished at the last end of the depression.

Old Fordson

Rubber Tire John Deere

Needed Trailer

On the other hand, the new rubber tired John Deere loved sand knolls and could pull the harrow and a drag attached with ease. Soon after this we bought a John Deere cultivating tractor to speed up our work and within a year the saddest day came to sell the ever-faithful horses. We knew that they would end up for meat food at the mink farms, ladies winter mink collared coats were the rage at this time so we sold the horses to another farmer who probably sold them for mink meat food, we never wanted to know what happened to them.

This was as drastic change on the farm life as my great grandfather experienced after selling the powerful oxen when the faster workhorses replaced them in the 1800's.

World War II had started and time became an important factor for the John Deere would only travel about 8 mph, so I had the idea of making a new needed trailer with a truck differential and by adding a transmission to it would then be able to save some time by pushing the tractor in neutral and tripling the speed, this was attached to the tractor power takeoff. The hand clutch and two wheel brakes on the tractor controlled the trailer. This could only be used after I had taken a load of apples to be unloaded in Lyndonville, just for coming five miles home. This improvised idea was ok but could have given me a peck of troubles with a jack knife effect. Ivor Kepner an arch welder made the trailer to perform my idea, and with his keen mind made it workable saving few traveling hours needed in World War II. 1944-45.

When I was out in the field working with this new rubber tired tractor that seemed so simple really was an ingenious piece of machinery. It had a large metal simple bar or lever as a hand clutch that when engaged could move you with the right gearing forward slow to fast or backwards. With the rubber tires it was so much easier to make a straight furrow and the two efficient cylinders aided by the flywheel gave it plenty of torque power and efficiency to finish a job. It just made life fun on the farm so fascinating like using a giant toy compared with the unfortunate drudgery the old ways had been.

The wheel made its meaningful entrance in the nineteenth century; you see these little flywheel engines running and huge steam engines being exhibited at Farm Festivals, they were used to run machinery, pull or pump water etc. before electricity became available. As I was driving the old steel wheel Fordson tractor with its wobbly steering it took all the strength I had to make a straight furrow, the change for this happened in my day. It was quite an experience from what my father did following a team of horses for me to ride and drive a spring loaded seat with a soft riding rubber balloon tired tractor. What an experience this was for me at my young age to have the privilege to make use of these new inventions! I no longer had to fight the steering; it glided over the bumps and could pull most all of the equipment to make a field fit to plant and then to harvest. It changed my thinking of living like doing the hard work my father had to do.

While in the field working with these inventions I had time to use my imagination. The past and the future even the 1824 Erie Barge Canal that actually divided our area into an island surrounded by water attached by bridges. There is still a remaining mule path east of Rochester where a part of the canal still remains to pull the barges and in my day waiting at a rising lift bridge seeing and hearing the chug, chugging of the steam or diesel tug with its rotating water propeller pulling tons of whatever to somewhere to be unloaded.

Maybe like the huge dirigible I saw when I was young that flew over the farm in the 1930's, now 2013 could be guided by satellite toward a given programmed delivery point. They could be used to carry tons of cargo above the costly highways and bridges that are in constant in repair. The canal could be drained and made into a super highway for rapid or for our personal family transportation across the State driven by remote guidance someday eliminating the costly antiquated lift bridges. This would put our state back as the Empire State as it should be.

One thing that bothers me inside is the changes in our way of life we are so fortunate to acquire from our ancestors. The philosophy of some of the new immigrants would like their culture to replace the time proven results we have inherited. We must not forget to look back and see what our freedom has become through these past centuries.

The farmers' sons and daughters today have told me some great stories they have accumulated while using the technology of the human minds put to work to use in the fields. Many times now talking to different farmer's grandsons, they have come and told me as I listened and understand their language what they are doing on his or her farm knowing as an example the amount of horsepower their tractors have and technical knowledge on the advanced scientific procedures that has a significant advancement beyond my recollections.

CHAPTER 12
True Farm Stories

PRAIRIE FIRE

One of our horses we named "Dick" we purchased came from the prairies and had gone through a prairie fire. He was nervous about fires so we tried to always have him on the far side when approaching the burning brush pile of trimmed apple limbs (later we made a brush pusher attached to the tractor). My brother Art tried to ride him bareback with only the bridle while I rode Max bareback up the lane. Dick was nowhere near the gentle horse that Max was, and was not appreciative of having Art on his back. Dick bucked him off and Art went flying over his head still hanging on to the bridle stapes. Surprisingly, Art ended up on his feet and Dick was at least gentle enough not to move saving Art from falling.

In the winter going up to the house for dinner we would hook our sleds to a spike on the back of the slide boat and have a fast ride back to the house. The horses knew that their oats, hay and water were there for their dinner and they were in a rush to get back. One of our horses name Fritz when coming back on a very cold day coughed, and broke a blood vessel and died in the stall, having bled to death.

HORSES RAN AWAY WITH THE STRANGER

I also remember a neighbor Ed borrowed our horses and wagon for something and coming back the horses ran away with him. I couldn't believe old Bill and gentle easy going Max would ever be that way. Dad and I yelled to Ed, "holler, whoa, whoa," but to no avail. Our horses sensed he was a stranger so didn't respond to his voice. The large pin released the whippet trees leaving the wagon. Ed ended in the ditch and the horses to return home to their masters.

MISTREATING MAX, A FRIENDLY HORSE

My brother Art and neighbor friend hooked up Max to the old buggy and went through the paths in the orchard. They threw apples at him to make him run faster, and well, he did. Galloping so fast the buggy became unhooked and Max came to the garden without the buggy right to Grandpa and me in the garden where we were picking vegetables for dinner. Grandpa said they probably ran into a tree. Grandpa said, "go see if they are all right." I ran to the orchard and sure enough the buggy had crashed into an apple tree. Knowing they had done wrong, my brother Art and his friend must have run to the nearby woods and hid. On Halloween night local boys hoisted a buggy up on the neighbor's outhouse for kicks.

HORSES FRIGHTENED THE COW

As an adult, while on my last call one afternoon, I took my two teen aged boys along to help. It was to a farm that had one cow to breed. The owner had tied her with a rope to the horse and cow feed bunk to confine her. As we approached the bunk the horses out in the pasture saw the owner come and thought they were being fed the grain. They started galloping towards the bunk frightening the cow. She was scared by them and took off with the feed bunk going end over end spilling the grain. The boys seeing this incident was an act they never forgot by picturing what had happened.

A BROKEN DRINKING CUP IN A FARMER'S BARN

Once, when I went to do an inseminating service at one of the farms on East High Street in Lockport, the cows were fastened in headlocks. Through the years the handy bailing string was used to keep the lock from opening. There wasn't any faucet to fill my pail with water so I had to press the available drinking cup to over flow in front of a cow for water to later wash and disinfect my boots. The cow was startled and lurched back breaking the strings in the lock. She backed out, the farmer not around my trying to put her back in place she jumped over the manger breaking off another drinking cup and the pressured water hit the ceiling and I couldn't find any valve to shut it off. They had a large Pit Bulldog in the house where the shut off valve was and it happened to be a very busy day with many more calls. As luck would have it, the farmer came home and rescued my predicament. There were some incidentals I can't forget traveling the back roads.

CHAPTER 13
Crops

Rotation was the key to production until commercial fertilizers became available. Grandpa, Dad and I sometimes if not in school, would attend meetings in the winter to learn best procedures to follow for pruning and growing new varieties of fruits and vegetables and using controlling sprays. They would plant oats in the spring; the ground would be worked loosely. Soon after they were thrashed waiting for the Hessian Fly free date around September 21st. We planted the field with winter wheat and as I can remember Dad would say, "work the ground real well," and it paid off.

We sowed alfalfa, ladino clover, and timothy grass seed in the early next spring on the growing wheat near the last frost to nourish and start the growing hay for the following year of the rotation

cycle on the winter wheat fields. It would be well established by the time we harvested the wheat. The gambrel roof barn was built in 1911 and was about fifty feet high at its peak. Late next spring we would cut the hay haul it to the barn and put it lose touching the rafters for the winter food supply. Turkey Buzzards arriving in the spring were always present to clean up dead animals or anything that had died especially along the roadsides. The following spring we planted field corn, followed by a cash crop like cabbage or tomatoes, potatoes, muskmelons, sweet corn and other money making crops, each year starting the routine all over again doing each plot in sequence. This would add nutrients to the soil the most profitable way. Manure was spread and plowed under to help loosen the soil and even up the PH level, I don't think we had a way of testing for the PH 7 level. Some crops added acid and some alkali to the land, the main reason for rotating. Legumes added nitrogen and sweetened the soil the vegetables used up.

Vegetables were next that gave me a sense of how we depend on the Supreme Being giving a magical conversion to transform things for our benefit. Growing potatoes was one of my favorites. Dad and I being a teenager, would be sitting near the barn door taking the Certified disease (scab) free seed potatoes that came from Prince Edward Island, Canada to produce a crop of saleable scab free potatoes for the market and looking for the eyes (sprouts) to make sure when we cut it in about four quarters each chunk would have had at least one eye. After each seedling was planted with the planter, it spaced them just the right distance apart on the sandy knoll. It was no time the sprouted eye broke through the ground with the warmth of the sun doing its miracles. Soon the vines blossomed to germinate the buried multiple new tubers then this always fascinated me. We had to use a spray called copper sulfate to control the blight. In Ireland it devastated their potato dependable crops and many of the residents migrated to the USA at that time. The excitement of digging up many full-grown potatoes from each hill was magical. We had no trouble finding young boys paying them five cents to fill a bushel basket. When tomatoes, cabbage, squash, etc. we grew to sell when cultivated all produced and the abundance to be sold or eaten.

When the ground warmed up to about seventy degrees in the spring my father would have the cabbage seed treated with something. I'm not sure, but I think it was formaldehyde to help control club root a disease that cabbage had. Without treatment it infected the soil and became another disaster to contend with. It was part of my duty to make sure the transplants were grown somewhere else on the farm, disease free ready, and the bushel baskets full of these little transplants spread out on wooden open containers fastened on the transplanter behind the tractor above the laps of the two very low opposite riders with a rhythm one on the right the other with the left hand for every other plant. By taking turns each would be spaced just right to have the maximum amount of soil for each plant to grow freely.

My daughters and sons keep reminding me of what the dusty, dirty job it was planting on my father and brother's farm to help pay for their college education. They would spend the first half of the day in the hot sun pulling bushel baskets of cabbage seedlings. The second half of the day they spent riding a two seat transplanter with a large fifty gallon tank full of water with a high nitrogen analysis fertilizer starter mix that flowed with a click to give the new plants a boost before the next rain to takeover for the growing season. The cabbage harvesting was about the last crop we did as the cold weather began. We had a weight scales with a bag holder so we filled each with the fifty pounds required; when we had enough we loaded the wagon and took them to the train depot where there were railroad cars waiting to be filled then shipped to the city.

Sometimes the price was very favorable and sometimes when it wasn't we would store it in our packing building hoping for a price rise, if it didn't rise within a month the cabbage soon began to rot. It was worse than the horse and cow waste and very slippery and mushy. Just "awful" is all I can say to clean out of the building that had to be done.

I can still visualize the rows full of red ripe tomatoes that filled the tomato baskets in the field acres. I loaded them on the wagon and took full loads to the drop off point located at where the scales were at the pea vinery. An inspector would take a couple of basket samples from a different location on the wagon to check for black rot and other defects and then give a rating for the quality of the load. We were given a slip for each load we brought and paid according to the inspector's ratings. The tomatoes went to the Heinz factory in Medina to be processed into canned tomatoes and catsup. To encourage the pickers my father sent me to the country store to buy half pints of packaged ice cream to give to the pickers on a hot summer or a fall day. My job was to do the loading and delivering and didn't do much of the picking. What a time to live from the planted unseen to the resulting spectacular we witnessed!

Manual labor income was at an all-time low in making enough to survive; today it has been replaced by machinery that does everything I have mentioned completely to the end product of producing milk, meat and other products, wrapped and many frozen for a quick meal.

It has put a strain on our Democracy and as we live longer and better. The younger generation is being put into a tremendous position of having to make more money to pay for survival. Both men and women are working full time to keep up with their bills and raising a family. We are getting to a point of not having enough time in the twenty four hours. The rule is eight hours for working and eight hours for recreation and pleasures eight hours for sleeping for a man to support his family. The women have entered the workforce resulting in the home care for the children is much more than she could handle. A time to live has become a question of where has the time gone in your life? I have found with this extended life it's not a healthy situation to be entertained all the time it becomes wasteful and boring for some. A good hobby helps to fill the gap.

CHAPTER 14
Summer Threshing

I was old enough to remember one of the first powerful tractors used to run the threshing machines with the two little balls that whirled around on the big steel wheel tractor called the governors that somehow would work in and out to give the proper power to the belt for constant speed. One extra bundle really made it bark and made me chuckle to hear the chugging power working. I watched as the bundles in the lofts were being emptied by the hired man and saw my father wringing wet with perspiration, a red handkerchief around both of their necks to keep the prickly chaff out on the very hot humid day in August. Farming in the 1930's and before was hard work but satisfying for the soul, I had a taste of it but welcomed the change. The scythes and homemade rakes still hung on the beams.

The roads being paved from the dirt and gravel now it was changing all equipment to rubber from the steel wheels for transporting. It was an exciting time to see the threshers enter the driveway. Even the dog seemed to know what was happening. It took all day to thrash out the wheat and oats so Mother had to cook the annual boiled pork and cabbage dinner the German threshers loved. We set up a washbasin outside for them to wash the accumulated dust off their faces and hands. What a time they had talking with each other in a little German about the local news while we all were eating. They had very hearty laughs to help settle their stomachs to break up the work to be done.

Going back after dinner to start up the thresher, first I want to tell a little about the horse drawn grain binder that cut the wheat or oat grain loaded bundles, tied them and threw them out on the ground. We would then pick them up and make little tent shapes with ten bundles of sheaves each in rows. The purpose of this was to let the sun dry the grain for threshing. After a week or so they would be taken to the barn and put up in the mows. They filled the barn loft almost to the rafters it was so high up I stayed down on the ground afraid of the height at my age. Each year as I grew older the threshing machine would come and the bundles would be pitched down to the threshing machine table, I soon was able to lift the sixty pound basket full of the shelled wheat grain, thirty two pounds when the lighter oats were threshed, as one basket was filled a lever on the machine was switched to the other basket, hurrying we would dump it into the grain bins then go back and trade the empty for a full one, wheat in one bin and, oats in the other. In the wheat bins we would climb in barefooted. I can still remember the experience feeling of the kernels between my toes as we spread and leveled it in the bin. Weevil larva sometimes got into the grain and cyanide would be used to fumigate the bins. Locks were put on the sliding doors for a certain length of time to prevent killing the pets or us.

Many times the threshers would pull the threshing machines out of the burning barns by the tractor's long drive belts that ran the machines. The barns were set fire by a stone going through the threshing machines and causing a spark that ignited the ever-present straw dust. By the time the fire trucks arrived the only thing they could save were the houses and out buildings.

Many started by putting in wet green hay in the lofts that wasn't quite sun cured and would heat up so hot that it would catch on fire. This was called spontaneous combustion. Many times we put in hay that wasn't quite dry because a storm was threatening and we had to take that chance otherwise the quality of the hay would be ruined for good feed. Dad would hand spread some salt in the mow to lessen the heating.

CHAPTER 15
Local Fires

Talking about fires reminded me of the numerous spectacular large barn fires. Some barns that burned during the depression years may have been set and burned to collect the insurance to pay off the farm debts, at least that is what my father thought. Many other fires had different causes, but all had the same impact on the families.

Walking distances from where I lived I witnessed a number of large mostly barn fires they were always spectacular, full of hay making large black smoke clouds you could see miles away. It brought out the farm people from miles around together watching the firemen do their duties to save what close by out buildings they could from the blazing hot flames.

OUR HOUSE almost went up in flames. When I was almost three years old and my brother was seven he decided to have a campfire in 1928. The location was a crawl space under the back porch. While my mother was washing the dishes she saw smoke rising very near the window. She went out to investigate and found my brother had built a little pile of leaves and wood pieces and had set them on fire with matches he had found. She discovered us pulled me out ran into the house grabbed the washbasin and doused the fire with soapsuds. So here I am today able to tell about the many country fires.

SCHNACLE'S barn down the road from the Todkill farm burned years earlier by a stone spark that ignited from the grain-thrashing machine. No one was hurt and the machine was saved by the tractor backing up with the belt still running and one of the thrashers steered it by the tongue far enough away to save the hard to replace machine from its important use to most farms in the area that time of the year. My mother told me about the first one very late in life.

GEORGE CORSER'S barn fire was one I can remember vividly because while it was burning, a crowd of neighbors gathered around to watch. There was a sulfur spray barrel next to the burning barn that got so hot it exploded into the air. It looked like a miniature atomic bomb going off. You never saw a crowd disperse so quickly, I was pushed down on the road and tore a hole in my new pants. The memory never left my thoughts.

CHAFFEE'S dairy barn at the corner burned on a windy day. A feed delivery truck that had stopped to unload cow feed caused this fire. A small stem of dried weed had touched the truck muffler starting the fire with a very small blaze but immediately spread through the dry grass to the barn siding and in no time it was engulfed with an uncontrolled fire burning the large barn up in a short time.

TODKILL'S large livestock barn was near the same corner next to the Lutheran Church on the July 4th a few years later. Some kids lit a fire cracker along the road that caught the grass on fire that raced across the field on a windy day to the barn and burned it down, I missed seeing that one.

APPLE DRY HOUSE burned years later. It employed quite a few part time women in the fall that needed the welcomed income for the necessities, this was located near the same corner another spectacular fire was started by a welding torch. I saw this happen while I was mowing the church lawn on a Saturday afternoon. I saw the whole building demolished. I didn't go to help it was all ablaze so quickly. Fire companies from everywhere arrived but the very dry wood in the building burned quickly. The near-by homes and grocery store were saved.

MY CHURCH was located next to the Dry House, County Line United Methodist Church. The church caught on fire in 1934 while I was in the country school next to the church. We looked out the window and watched the firemen come to put out this fire and a couple of daring men went inside laid on the basement floor and got it under control to extinguish. It did a lot of damage and the above flooring had to be replaced in the sanctuary. It started from the janitor who left the draft opened on the wood burning furnace and the stovepipe became so hot it started on fire right near the chimney. The church experienced a second fire in the 1990's and was discovered by a passing feed truck. He blew his horn to alert a neighbor who called the fire companies. We think the sparrows that had built their nests in back of the lighted outside Cross, shorted the electric wires caused this. A group of parishioners including the minister gathered around to watch and a small group of us including myself saw a smoke silhouette that appeared to be like a human male face next to the outside Cross. We all said it did look convincing for a second.

DUNHAM'S chicken coup across from my farmhouse caught on fire by the black kerosene heater that kept the baby chicks warm. Using up the oxygen I guess caused it to explode. Later his barn burned burning up his car and while I was there one of the fire trucks went into the barnyard broke the front tie rod that held the wheels straight and it provided quite a lot of excitement to pull it away from the burning barn on the frozen ground.

MY GRADE SCHOOL FRIEND'S HOUSE who lived across from the Somerset Cemetery fell to the flames. My friend and his family occupied the apartment above the garage with the door opened below. Frank from Bridgman Oil was delivering gasoline to an outside fuel tank. The fumes drifted in and when the owner George came to talk to Frank he lit his cigar and the house exploded into flames. Some of the family perished, this was an unexpected tragedy for the Somerset community of 1938.

VILLAGE of LYNDONVILLE When I was about ten years old I can remember my father saying, "Gordon hop in the car the whole village of Lyndonville is on fire!" You could almost see the fire five miles away. The atmosphere made a glow in the sky that was indescribable. We were speeding east in the 1929 Chevy down the Yates Center dirt road when in a short time an orange moon came up and fooled us with its glow. There wasn't really any fire at all. Nature has its way to fool you.

VILLAGE of BARKER had a fire that I can remember at the Canning Factory. When I was very young, the fire burned and all the labels on the pound cans off, so they were giving away the canned foods. We were given four cans they probably were peas but we didn't know until we opened them. At different times the Cold Storage, the McAdam Farm Machinery building, one end of Dry Goods Store and Grocery Store, and the Laundromat were some buildings that burned. These fires hurt the downtown business and haven't been replaced but the ones that have survived are still are doing ok with pleasant surroundings. The Village Park, Library, Post Office, restaurants, very well equipped volunteer Fire Company, Bank, School, Refueling Station with a Deli, an excellent and active Town Park with all kinds of sport events, few other Clubs with their support and churches help to keep the village identity strong and friendly.

CHAPTER 16
Huge Straw Stack

The straw used for bedding the stock was blown into the barnyard reaching as high as the top of the barn roof. My friends and I made tunnels in the clean fresh straw for hiding places when we played games before the stack settled. The cows and horses would run around it wearing a groove that made an overhang loving the back rubs. It also made a perfect place for the sparrows to make their nests using the chicken feathers and string from the empty feed bags for a cozy home during the winter.

As time went on a friend of my Dad had a new John Deere Combine that would thrash our grain in the field, separate it and put in the burlap feed bags. I would ride on the little platform and my father taught me how to tie them with a millers knot. Then the full bags were loaded in the field and taken to the barn granary, this was in the 1940's. I bought a new six-foot John Deere Combine for our farm pulled by the John Deere tractor in 1950. It had a big hopper for the grain. When filled we would stop and elevate into a portable bin on the pick-up truck and take it to the granary, a much faster and easier way to thrash the wheat and oat grains. The summer before we were married in 1951, Nancy would come out from the city for a romantic ride on the John Deere tractor pulling the combine. This must have been a first for a way of courting; sure made it fun to have her riding with me while working. The straw was tied in bales by a baling machine in the field and put up in the barn mows, no more straw stacks, less sparrows with nice cozy homes.

The pea harvesting machines are high on my lists of inventions right now. Why? Because on the farm we grew peas and found the labor of harvesting the peas was very hard work. We cut the pea vines pitched them onto the wagon, hauled them down to the pea vinery, fork pitched the twisted vines off where they were shelled, then were taken by a truck to Birds-Eye in Medina, NY to be processed and frozen. Now huge machines come into a large field of peas and cuts, separates the peas from the pods puts them into a hopper unloads them to a moving dump wagon then to a waiting semi-trailer truck full to the freezer plant, with no manual labor except driving the expensive efficient equipment. The peas were frozen quickly giving the public almost fresh peas from the fields. No more hand blisters pitching pea vines.

There are so many machines now that have changed the way farming is being done compared to my past experiences. There was one I never forgot it was the new corn shelling machine, it worked great for doing the shelling but the waste stalks were blown into the barn yard that became twisted, wet and trampled by the cows and horses. When it came to cleaning the barnyard forking this waste was another time-consuming problem it was like tangled rope or a twisted extension cord that had to be removed. It soon proved to be the machine we could forget for its purpose until the self-propelled combines entered its debut shelling the corn and distributed the chopped stalk waste back on to the field to be plowed under to enrich and aerate the clay soil, no more hand forking for me.

This was another reason for the beginning of the exodus of the small family farms crossed New York State and the country that may never be the same as it had been for the past one hundred and fifty years or more, gone and the land sold to the larger landowners. This changed the foresight to the wild animals and birds that lived on our farm. Rooster pheasants had so decreased we farm boys and our dogs that loved to hunt were out of luck for the sport during the hunting season. The shotguns were put away and left idle, most of the hiding places for the birds are gone. The all-purpose dogs now are only pets.

CHAPTER 17
Farm Friends

The hardest thing to do on the farm was to be the one to bury a faithful dog that grew old and became too feeble to be  useful. That was the way in those days. It was burying your best friend you learned to love in just a few short years. A cute puppy was saved from an English Shepherd female that was given to us. She had a litter of eleven; we kept one and named him Piper because his white markings on the back of his neck had a shape like a man's corncob pipe. We sold the rest of the litter.

All were very intelligent and easy trained to do different farm jobs they were told to do. We gave the mother away to someone. Each time we would go to the field, we would take Piper. He soon learned that when we said, "Go get the cows!" he would know what we wanted him to do. It wasn't long before he could be on his own and go up to the farthest field and bring the cows back to the barn each early morning and late afternoon to be milked. Piper's other duties were watching the open gates, getting the chickens inside the fence or maybe going pheasant hunting. He was our playmate too. Whether it was just playing around with us or going with us swimming down to Lake Ontario on a hot summer evening, he always provided us with lots of fun.

Cats were plentiful around the farm and their job was to control the mouse and rat population that were always eager to clean up the spilled ground grain. The cats weren't allowed in the house. When finding where the mother cat had hid her kittens in the barn she would move them by carrying them by the neck to another hiding place. If not found before they could run, the kittens became quite wild and were hard to catch and tame. Kittens were adorable but sometimes a stray tomcat would come over and kill them. I guess it was nature's way of controlling overpopulation. Some would die of a disease called distemper. Tomcat fights were furious and would go on for days; hearing their screeches gave me the chills.

There were other favored animals on the farm that occupied our some of our time. Rabbits were other pets that were favorites in my life. I was given an empty horse stall and an old door to make a rabbit pen. I sold a few to friends and for a while had good luck with them. I soon found them more bother to keep clean than they were worth, besides I was getting into more school activities. We raised a few Mascovy and Pekin ducks that had the run of the back yard they provided a meal or two. My brother had a ewe sheep he would take a round stake and pound it in the ground and fasten a long chain to her collar so she could eat the grass around the buildings. You had to keep your eye on her because she had a mean bunt to protect her pair of twin lambs that were so helpless but were full of energy. That makes life on the farm so meaningful of what has been created.

We had some animals on the farm we didn't like too. Mostly animals that were around to clean up the spilled grain or find shelter to make a home for their families. I can't call them pests but we did. The skunks ate the lawn grubs, the rats ate the spilled grain, the woodchucks seemed to munch on the grass that was missed with the lawnmower and the owls and hawks were after the mice for their meals out in the fields. The harmless grass snakes in the garden sometimes found a way into our house. In more recent years of our homestead, my ninety year old mother lived alone in the homestead. One day she called me frantically said a snake about three feet long had found its way to the top of her electric stove and was resting right on the burners. Petrified of snakes, she had put an old flat iron on it before I arrived. I took it to the woods and released it.

CHAPTER 18
Bird Farm Friends

I am thinking about the birds that were at the farm and the ones that came back for the warm season to help us out with their beauty, their songs and the work they did to make country life much more pleasant. I'm amazed at the number of birds we had there.

Why do they come back year after year to be so helpful with their presence? On the farm it isn't just working the hard labor with plenty of sweat running off your backs, it's much more to observe your surroundings and think why we are here to provide food for others.

BARN SWALLOW

These fine-feathered friends gave me the answers right before my eyes. They too are here to build their nests and raise a family, but must provide the food that has been provided in abundance. The alfalfa and sweet clover in the fields and other related plants we planted the seeds to depend on become infested with insect weevils that could destroy a much needed winter food supply for the livestock to carry over to the next year.

BARN SWALLOWS: These dive-bombers are on the prowl daily from daylight to almost darkness to invade these pests to provide food for their young. While walking up the cow path I experienced the most interesting facts of why they come back. There must be a supreme being on earth that puts everything in its place for all to be here in a time to live.

Recently, I was sitting in my garage with both overhead doors open. In flew a Barn Swallow not looking for insects at the present, but maybe a place to build their mud nest to raise a family. Within a few warm days the insects will hatch out and the timing to feed the hatched out babies with their bills wide open puts the parents to work.

On the farm from April through September the insects like barn flies laid their eggs becoming ugly maggots, which always turned me off but had a purpose of eating up the waste behind the farm animals if we didn't clean twice daily. It made me realize the important work of the food chain purpose also becoming flies for baby swallows food.

The barn doors were left open through this season making it a perfect place for the swallows to build their muddy nests every year on the hand hued cross beams that were up high enough for the new babies to be away from harm from the farm cats below.

The swallows were quite a tame bird to humans flying close by while bringing the insect food to the newborns. Great uncle Charlie Hall was an engraver for the US. Mint and also an artist and was a bird enthusiast. He told me when he was visiting that these swallows caught enough insects to equal their own weight every three hours during daylight hours. Their mouths were designed and shaped like a wide scoop. This I could believe because when out in the fields mowing hay that would stir up different insects they would fly around the equipment dashing around almost impossible flights very close to me with their unbelievable flight angles catching the meals for the young ones.

Being in the barn where we did a lot of work like packing apples in bushel baskets, we had to work clear of the swallow nest because the wastes would be dropped. That was messy but we all as well as our relatives appreciated these birds because in the late afternoon the mosquitoes would be anxious for our blood. While we sat under the big old horse chestnut tree in the front yard, these birds were welcomed friends in the summer months to keep the insects at bay. What a bird! Not many barn doors are left open any more for nesting and now I have been seen less frequently.

KINGBIRDS (EASTERN): These were great to have around. They too caught insects especially along the roadsides and many were killed being hit by the fast moving traffic on the highways. I don't know much about these birds except seeing those catching insects because I was on the highway every day. Where they nested was up to the bird watchers for this.

PURPLE MARTINS: I had a martin house for a while filled with martins for a few years, but I think the insect food may have been cut back because the village where I lived had an insect spray-fogging program during the summer seasons that may have limited their food supply. When we went to Lake Ontario they were in their glory with the small dead fish that washed up on the shore back in those days where the gnats-flies were feasting they seemed to be happy with their food supply. Living in colonies, they liked to be together with maybe four or more families in one birdhouse. Having a good home brought them back, their flights were fun to watch could almost turn right angles catching insects. When their tummies were full it was quite a sight to see them lined up on the power and telephone wires as if discussing when will it be time to be going south for the winter?

TREE SWALLOWS: I had these in my back yard a few summers another dashing bird insect catcher. They had an iridescent bluish green back fluorescent cast and a little smaller than barn swallows.

CHIMNEY SWALLOWS (Swifts): We have those around most of the summer, they flap their wings very rapidly and have what appears to be a stubby tail. I suppose they also feed their young with the insects. I never saw them around the barns but more above the old homestead house.

YELLOW BIRDS (American Goldfinch): They were seen in our pasture where the grass, thistles, dandelions, buttercups and daisies blossomed. I welcomed these spring birdies that came to the farm.

BLUEBIRDS: One of the treats walking up the lane on the cow paths was to see the bluebirds on a fence post that had a rotted knothole that some had making a perfect place for a protected nest. This was such a delight to see their blue feathers and the reddish colored breast. Before dark they would rest on the telephone wires and gave the most glorious song. I wish my hearing were better because now I'm missing most all these solos. They feasted on the larvae and insects.

BOBOLINKS: When I went bare-foot with the dog to get the cows the mixed black and white bobolinks were resting on top of the tall weeds giving its song bob-o-link a happy tune that stays with me from so many years ago. I haven't seen one in a long time because many of the small field farms with line fences to raise their families have disappeared.

MEADOWLARKS: I wish I could hear them but they have almost vanished. I painted them in some of my paintings and can remember what a bird they were and again near the lane where I walked. They knew I wouldn't harm them so I got pretty close to all these different birds.

Most everyone that has bird feeders never get these country farm birds so this kind of living just has changed. They are still around maybe but the old cow paths and lanes where you might say the guided bird tour is gone. It was a time to live.

CHICKADEES: They come to my bird feeder all winter. I see these cute little guys but the real thrill is to have them right next to you in an apple tree we would be trimming.

I would see these in the cold winter on a sunny day even though it was cold but you could feel the sun's heat coming through the clear sky. It is hard to describe the freshness in the air that you can breathe when outside working in the orchards. They were going up and down the limbs probably seeking the codling moth eggs that end up in wormy apples left on the trees. We kept up our ten-day spraying intervals starting in the spring using lead arsenic to produce the quality fruit to sell. No matter how we tried the insects had a way to multiply faster than the poisons we were using could get rid of them. The chickadees did their best and so did we to grow fruit to ship to the market but it was a constant battle.

There are many other small birds that are still around I haven't mentioned but these also were helpers on the farm not freeloaders like some that thrived on spilled grain. After making this last statement I found that most all birds are beneficial in some way.

The starlings are also on the lawns daily feasting on grubs. The chip sparrows are at the feeder but I also see those catching moths. The Downey and Ladder Back woodpeckers like the suet and are regular visitors but they too get most of their food knocking on the trees getting the insects that do a lot of damage and in some cases kill the trees. My beautiful white birch in the front yard was a victim. So again my statement about some birds being freeloaders can be disputed.

KILLDEER BROOD

KILLDEER: These birds live very dangerously; They lay their eggs amongst a few pebbles I'd say not even should it be called a nest along a driveway or some ridiculous place. I don't know their reasoning. To protect their nest they have a way of distracting by putting on an act of being wounded like a broken wing to lure you away from the nest. As soon as her chicks are hatched they themselves are capable of finding insects maybe ants for food. I marvel at their way to survive yet still see them return every summer. They have a penetrating alert cry and I guess whoever named them "killdeer" heard the warning. Other animals respect nature's way of privacy.

BATS: Bats are animals that fly but small like the birds we see every evening in the summer. We had small bats that came out in the twilight catching insects. My brother and I would throw little pebbles up in the air and they would dive thinking they were insects. One got into the homestead when (mother) Grandma Ruth lived alone and called me to get it out of her bedroom. It got caught in the curtains so I could catch it and release it. They too were also useful. Something about them they always put a Halloween edgy fear into you. Some bats become rabid so caution has to be considered in handling these creatures.

Now visiting the farm there is hardly a place for those precious creatures to make a nest. Darwin had some good points but as these magnificent fliers with indescribable colors were right close by it is not hard for me to believe the whole story, could you?

CHAPTER 19
Farm Animals

Horses lived to fifteen or so years and were kept as long as they were useful like other animals on the farm. Chickens however, would be replaced each year for peak production. We had to vaccinate them for Newcastle disease, which was done by the veterinarian. It was done under the wing in a vein. Art and I would catch each hen for this procedure. I suppose this was done because we sold hatching eggs. Male pigs we castrated using a razor blade. They grew fast on the separated skim milk and were sold weighing about two hundred fifty pounds. Two were kept and butchered in the winter. By adding salt crystals to fat pork it preserved it and was put in a covered clay crock with a heavy stone on top. It added delicious meat to the baked beans. I didn't care for the pig butchering process; knives were for men to use. By the time I became a man we took the animals to the slaughtering house to be butchered. The handy estimated weight chart was used to determine the size by measuring the heart girth in inches without using the scales that gave us the approximate reasonable size knowing the

pigs that weighed about two hundred and fifty pounds was the desired growth for marketing. It was this premium weight we tried to have for the best quality cut of meat the markets preferred to sell to their customers.

My father gave me a calf to be raised for a 4-H project so I turned the pen into a calf stall. Our herd was all Registered Guernsey's and she was a great lot of fun to be around. Mother forbids having a bull on the farm and a female (heifer) at sixteen months of age was time for her to become a mother. The charts showed the approximate weight by her heart girth, at 64 inches or about 760 pounds, it was time for her to be led down the road two miles to a farm that had a Registered Guernsey bull to be mated for pregnancy. This proved to be a memorable experience for me at the age of fourteen. As I was leading my heifer down the side of the road toward home, the neighbor's large black and white bull jumped the fence. With his urge to perform, he partially knocked down the fence and wanted to mount my beautiful young tan and white registered heifer. I had just spent some of my savings for the breeding fee at the other farm and it would be a possibility for canceling out my intentions of having a purebred mating. Well, she being in estrus, I had prevented the unwanted mating with a sudden twist on the rope and got my heifer running up the road with the big brute following in pursuit and managed to get her home safely without the dreadful thoughts of who sired my prized animal.

All the milking cows were taken to the bull for breeding two months after they had calved. Two months near the end of her milking lactation she was dried off (stopped milking her) from giving milk; it was an important rest period before giving birth for the next calving. Through genetic breeding and improved feeding formulas it has become quite common for a cow to give twenty thousand pounds of milk each year, that is about forty thousand eight ounce glasses of milk from one lactation cycle each year if my math is right. In my experience it's amazing that many no longer have a breakdown in their udders to hold so much weight in milk, also instead of twice a day, they were put on a three time every eight hour milking schedule in the high producing herds. Through planned genetic breeding it is important to have four-quarter uniform positions for the milking machines to function properly.

This is some different than the days when I would milk two cows and my father milked the other three by hand twice a day and it had to be done every day. We did make it a practice to do everything we could to produce the best for our own health as well as for our regular customers. We didn't have any refrigeration but we seemed to have had a good way to use the fresh milk for our meals and cooking that had been practiced in the past.

When our local friends had guests come up from New York City one was about my age. He came to see how we did things on the farm and he was completely unfamiliar with where the milk he drank even came from other than the delivery milkman in the city. My father gave him a stool and a milk pail and told him to milk "Brownie" our gentle, loving older milk cow. He sat on the stool looked under the milking area and asked where he could turn on the spigot to get the milk. Of course we laughed and soon after manipulating a few pulls he did get a stream but he soon gave up and I took over to finish Brownie's faithful filling in the milk pail. Many who buy farm products at the grocery store haven't had the opportunity to know where the food originates, as long as it's available who cares?

Now with milking; everything is so automatically systemized, with stainless steel, regularly sanitized and almost instantly cooled and some have the milk as it flows into the cooler will go through a heat exchanger extracting some of the heat using a heat pump to heat hot water. In my opinion it's absolutely one of the best food products money can buy. These advances show up printed on the milk containers a much longer extended date for its freshness if kept refrigerated.

We had eight Registered Guernsey's, five were milkers. We sold raw milk to the neighbors and cream to the creamery. The skim milk from the separator was fed to the pigs. In the winter we put frozen ice in a sack and crushing it with the blunt side of an axe adding rock salt and in a cranked mixer we made homemade ice cream with plenty of rich cream. It was absolutely delicious. Dad and my Uncle Don would make it for church ice cream socials and band concerts, getting the ice from the cold storage in Lyndonville in the fall. A lot of the whipping cream was sold for added toppings on pies or fruit sauces this was raw milk most all consumed. The good bacteria from the raw milk may have helped put up a resistance for better health I believe, but many think differently. With pasteurizing we still have diabetes and other non-genetic diseases we take the antibiotics for that do away with the good and the bad bacteria's that are prevalent in most all of us. We still have a lot to learn how to take advantage of the unknown rather than the added chemicals we take.

The bull calves were suckling (bob-calves) until they weighed 200 lbs. about 40 inch heart girth and then sold for veal in just a few weeks, it was a good way to dispose of them and make a profit. Our horse barn and cow barn were near each other so the manure could be piled together. In the winter a slide boat would be loaded and drawn to the orchards and manure was forked around each tree. Mice found it made a nice home and when they were hungry, would girdle around the base of the trees for food survival.

CHAPTER 20
Church Festivities

English, other nationalities, and some Germans that intermarried into the church families attended the County Line Methodist church. Annual carnivals were the main source of raising money to support the church.  We had a greased pole with a Westclox pocket watch attached at the top for a prize. It was comical to see young men trying to climb up to get it. The pole was an ash sapling with the bark peeled off. Pillow fights on over-size saw horses were well used to challenge anyone to be knocked off. The ladies-aid women made the pillows of goose feathers. The prize was a baby duckling or rooster chick donated by the local Thiel's Hatchery for the one who didn't get knocked off the sawhorse, the winner was challenged by another winner. For a number of years there were parades, band concerts, concession stands, popcorn, homemade ice cream and other attractions for the crowds (at least two hundred or more). All these festivities helped make it a huge success. I was one of the boys who carried out the chairs.

One of the struggles in the 1930's was to keep everyone fed and happy. The church filled that void with plenty of volunteer activities. Money was scarce for all the rural people and the ones that were more successful helped to make the community a pleasant place to live by thinking up ways they could make up ideas and donating food for the suppers. I can remember the men would sit on the sidelines in the wooden folding chairs discussing the events of the day. We all knew they were having a good time you could tell by their laughter.

The rural community practiced these events as a good example for all to follow. Supporting the church activities with good morals of honesty without the raffles that has become for many a way of life of chance to win a fortune with the greatest odds. Some of the poor are the frequent players of hope for a better future that keep donating their hard earned money of the losing art of ruin by chance.

Penny suppers were another way of raising money for the church. A spoonful of each dish cost a penny. A good well-balanced meal could be purchased for about twenty-five cents and it would be enough to fill you up; the cost of living was much different then. Labor was 10 cents to 50 cents an hour. Donated home baked goods from the world's best cooks were always a sellout. Pantomime plays were put on for entertainment. Two white sheets were used as curtains strung on a wire with a spotlight behind. Actors behind the sheets would make silhouette images while someone would read a gruesome story, and the actors behind would act it out, with some sounds of fake pain. It sure brought a thought of discomfort or a lot of laughter. Anything to take away the drudgery of working was a great help after a long week of manual work.   It was usually a bloodthirsty story similar to a Frankenstein tale. The reactions from the audience came more from their imaginations than what the shadows they were seeing on the curtain.

Halloween in the 1930's was always a fun time at church. One of the activities that was fun was dipping your face in a tub of water to retrieve an apple with your teeth. Musical chairs, beanbag relays and other things added to the fun.   There were always the pranks of the young men that would go out in the community tipping over the toilets (outhouses). It turned out to be the annual time for all to clean the waste out, something that had to be done anyway. I have attended this church my entire life.

New additions to local barns were built by the owners who would sponsor square dances with local fiddlers and drummers for the public, at a small fee. This was a great way to pay for the barn raising. The hayloft made a perfect dance floor with its strong new tongue boards to hold the tons of hay for the next early summer harvest.

They all had to climb a ladder up there and I was young and scared of the height looking down when I went up.

CHURCH FIRES   Millers was a small community of about twenty homes with a train depot, temporary fruit and vegetable storages near the R.R. tracks, a grocery store and packing houses and an evaporator for pressing the juice out of apples to be fermented into vinegar a thriving business along the Lake Ontario fruit belt. The Methodist church that stood on the corner before my time burned. It was told that some men were playing cards inside and tipped over the lamp, that may have been a rumor, anyway it was destroyed and not rebuilt.

Our present Methodist church was built in 1852 about a mile and a half north on the Orleans side of the Niagara-Orleans County Line. In 1934 I can remember looking out of the country school window watching the firemen come and save the building from being destroyed by an overheated furnace. The scorched timbers are still visible in the basement dining room that is covered over with the added false ceiling.

In 1994 a Christian Cross with a lighted backing shorted out during a rainstorm. The sparrows had made their comfortable nests there and maybe somehow could have started on fire but it was discovered in the nick of time for the local firemen to come and saved it from another close disaster.

The horse sheds, where we played hide and seek, were torn down and towed away. I still have a horseshoe I found that appeared when the parking lot was being resurfaced for a welcomed parking area. The killdeer birds other years built their so-called nests of pebbles right in the middle of the parking lot where cars parked on Sundays. They had a way of letting you know so we put up an old chair as a decoy near it to avoid a disturbance for her to carry on her way. They have survived but how is a sure guess, when the chicks hatched out they immediately are able to seek food similar to baby chickens.

CHAPTER 21
Seasonal Activities

Apple wood was plentiful and used for fuel for heating and cooking. The old trees were cut down; the large limbs were placed into a pyramid shape to dry to produce less creosote to be buzzed up into one and a half foot lengths for the wood stoves. This was always a neighborhood event. The buzz saw was a round 3-foot

blade with teeth that were kept razor sharp. I can still sense the shriek of the blades as they sped through each chunk. The tractor was used with a long belt to turn it at high speed. I never liked to help with this operation because everything was rushed to get it cut up and it scared me. Many farmers lost one or two fingers doing this. The wood was taken to the back yard and piled in neat rows. The larger chunks would be split with a sharp ax and put with the rest to make the abundant fuel needed for cooking and heating.

Growing our own popcorn added some routine refreshments and in the winter Dad would open up the wood and coal furnace in the cellar, and using a screened popper, shake, and presto a full batch of delicious popped corn came up from the cellar then it was mixed with lots of creamery butter and salt and with peeled Northern Spy apples, it was our Sunday evening treat. Popcorn balls were special treats along with homemade milk chocolate fudge filled with homegrown English walnuts and homemade ice cream made with real cream; we never got fat on the rich diets. The added can of pineapple brother Art liked or milk chocolate syrup I liked was the very best even compared by today's experts. We appreciated things like this because of the hard work that went into making these treats, which weren't available in packages like they are now. Doing it together made it a lot more pleasurable because it was a special event, sometimes after choir practice or card parties, the large trays or bowls full would be devoured in a jolly time.

The treats after rehearsals or at the parties were pretty well the same each time. The grape juice was made in the fall and preserved in glass jars with a rubber seal and by putting it in the large glass pitcher plus adding ginger ale gave it a little refreshing fizz. I sometimes wonder now about people's diets that steer away from these treats that we never seemed to put on the added weight, so many try to wear off by exercising. I guess we had enough physical work to keep us on the thin side. At the 4-H Camp for a week my new made friends called me "Spike," I wondered why? We appreciated things like this and it really made an evening of companionship working together ending the day and a week of remembrance to again look forward for the next time.

My brother Art and I did have many good times playing in the band. The band trips were our source of fun away from the farm. We almost never took trips during these times with very little extra income and besides we were committed to the routines of the daily chores. Dad did take us to the Barnum and Bailey Circus once. This gave us ideas for fun. In the front yard of the tenant house where our family lived we used the large hay ropes for very wide swings fastened between two maple trees in the front yard with a pull rope and a down filled pillow. We did acrobatic maneuvers that made my mother look the other way from being upset with our dare devil stunts.

We rode our bikes to Lyndonville and I remember going into large tents, it was called "Chautauqua" that had great ideas for the youth with free entertainment all day. One thing that impressed me was making a large clay jar on a potter's wheel that looked exactly like grandma's cookie jar. Neighbor friends would come to our lawn and we played softball or touch football and were treated with a molasses cookie with a raisin on top. Sometimes we'd go to the woods to climb the wild grape vines or look for wheels, baby buggy springs, etc. in the junk pile for something to bring back to make maybe a little bike trailer at the barn tool shop.

We really celebrated July 4th in the 1930's with cap guns and firecrackers. In the evening at the end of our road at the lake, the Shirt Factory owner had enough money at the adjoining property to give us the annual treat by providing fireworks of Roman candles and loud bangs that were fun to watch showing their displays over the lake. We biked to the lake many times to skip stones, and when the water was calm and warm enough, we went swimming. There was a creek outlet nearby for fishing by taking a can with angleworms we had dug up for bait. We fished for the jack perch with the long bamboo pole with a strong string a bobber and a hook. The waiting game for a bite sometimes tried our patience and we headed home.

For some real excitement when Dad took us to the Niagara County Fair sitting in the Grand Stand watching Dare Devil Lucky Teeter with his 1935 Dodge two door sedan automobiles noisy without their mufflers. They would tip and balance riding on two wheels a real trick. Then racing down the track going up a ramp high enough to jump over a couple of cars landing on the opposite ramp gave us kids' ideas when we got home.

We soon made for our bikes large rubber bands from a discarded punctured car's tire inner tube, we'd stretch it across the handlebars and by traveling fast it would vibrate by the wind sounding like a motor. With some sawhorses and old doors we made ramps for our bikes to fly through the air and sometimes missing the opposite ramp landed and bent the front wheel spokes. We always had replacement parts lying around to keep us motivated. We think kids today do crazy things, but what we did was just as daring.

Being so far out in the country and near the lake there wasn't much auto traffic during the working day so we had the road almost to ourselves. Our parents were very informative to emphasize road safety and if we were caught not using caution we lost that privilege and they locked up our bikes so we couldn't ride. We soon learned our lesson not being able to bike for a few days. In the winter we would go down to Lover's Lane where there was a decent hill to do tobogganing on the snow covered hill.

There was a small drainage ditch and a small stream of water that flowed in the winter in back of our big gambrel roof barn. After a snow storm some melted and the stream overflowed flooding into a neighboring field then froze hard enough to ice skate on or get a run with a sled do a belly flop and glide quite a ways down near the cemetery where the water had to flow though a bridge under the highway in the spring. It provided a lot of fun during the weekends with my friends to see how far we could coast and see who could go the farthest.

We never lacked some kind of fun on the farm and as long as we behaved the local farmers hardly ever complained about our trespassing, so we had a freedom that many kids lacked living in the cities. They must have had some fun I suppose too. Some cousins would come out and show us how to play hockey or play a good game of softball at the summer reunions with picnics on a holiday. A good frozen pond brought many country kids together and sometimes we would make a bonfire with some logs dragged in for seats to warm our feet. Cold weather was welcomed on a quiet day but when the wind blew it was game time playing hide and go seek in the barn with its numerous hiding places.

In the early spring when the trimming was completed the brush under the trees would be forked out between the rows and then loaded on a slide boat, taken to the end the orchard, put into a large pile and burned. In the winter going up to the house for dinner we would hook our sleds to a spike on the back of the slide boat and have a fast ride back to the house. The horses knew that their oats, hay and water were there for their dinner and they were in a rush to get back.

I went with my father to Nesbitt's a horse dealer and looked over a number of horses checking their teeth for some of the knowledgeable reasons selected and bought Max a young gentle, loving animal weighing about sixteen hundred pounds that would communicate his natural way being well broken to become part of the working force needed on the farm to perform his strength with everything he had to give daily. His temperament could be trusted and responded by our command in the most difficult circumstances. I was too young to really get acquainted with Old Fritz but Max was the best horse I've ever known.

CHAPTER 22
Entertainment

In the winter months square dances were held at Grange Halls for the teenagers with round and squares, the good beat orchestras kept us active with the added square dance callers instructing the sets of four couples to swing and twirl with the allemande lefts, doing this with a partner was so much fun. Roller-skating at a large rink at Shadigee north of Lyndonville became a Saturday or Sunday night activity for fun too. Radio programs after school were series broadcasts each day. "The Lone Ranger," "Jack Armstrong the All American Boy," "Dick Tracy," "Orphan Annie," and others were faithfully listened to. The chores were done in a hurry so we wouldn't miss the next episode. World Series baseball was a live broadcast with Babe Ruth and Dizzy and Daffy Dean the favorites.

I remember listening to an Orson Welles broadcast on the radio that really upset everyone. He said Martians were wading up the Hudson River and destroying everything in their paths. I can remember my dad saying where can we go, maybe to the lake to

escape, I thought what good would that do? To me it seemed that the this real live drama lasted for hours. Soon the realistic program ended and we all realized it was just a made-up story. The whole listening audience fell for the superior acting. The old crank telephones were buzzing, with everyone listening in because all rings were heard on the party line. All were scared to death for hours many that were on our line spread the news; all would lift up their receivers and listen, no privacy back then. Orson Welles' program was talked about for many years, and made him famous. Only in the USA could this practical joke be played on the public.

TELEVISION, NEW APPLIANCES, AND COMMUNICATIONS: In 1939 Art and I went to the New York World's Fair. We were invited to visit some friend's home on Long Island. These friends came to visit the County Line backcountry for a summer vacation. They had passes to the World's Fair so we could get in free to see the fascinating exhibits that our national industries had provided. They lived very close to the railroad station that would drop us off at the fairgrounds in no time. The demonstrations of many appliances were so futuristic; dishwashers, refrigerators with an icemaker, electric stoves, washing machines that spun the clothes dry instead of running them through a hand cranked rubber ringer and then hung on a full clothes line to dry every Monday.

We saw the first six-inch TV with President Roosevelt giving a message along with the well-known radio news commentator Lowell Thomas in a tent at the fair. The evening news was broadcasted on the radio in our living room home. When World War II started, most everyone had a radio and heard the news. I think later one of the appliances that fascinated me the most, and still does, was the color TV broadcast I saw at the County Fairs. We just had to have one, and now, in today's world, we have a couple others too. I am now reviewing more new advances called digital, high definition TV with not even a picture tube but a clear colored picture a size you want to view for a price you can afford and even hang it on a wall. It's incredible is all I can say. There is an occasional argument with the remote control for what we like to see and how loud to have the volume up for my fading hearing.

CHAPTER 23
Musical Training By the Masters

Our country schoolteachers we had were all single females. They had a tough time with the eighth grade boys at the country school like Smitty, a devil. The teacher, Miss Genevieve, chased him up and down the aisle, and he raised the window jumped out and ran home. My parents wouldn't stand for this they were always on the teacher's side it seemed when it came to discipline.

There was very little musical training so you see why I have kept repeating myself over and over because many students in our rural area were not having this opportunity. So an exit of the rural single country school rooms and becoming a centralized school to be better educated was a better way, not by one teacher teaching for all of the eight grades, but by a single teacher for each subject with the whole class passing or moving from one room to another being taught each subject on a given school day. This gives the extra tools provided for its specialized training. Eventually, they offered professional teachers for each school to enhance their lives to be prepared for the demanding advances to further education.

I was in the fifth grade at the country school and my mother wanted brother Art and I to have a better musical education. The school at Barker had a great award-winning band under the direction of Charles Barone and understanding the benefits. The next school year of 1937, my brother and I became band members in the school band. We didn't have a music room for instrumental training in the 1911 school for the sectional group lessons. Instead, we had to cross the street into a private home living room for this, and at this crossing the highway there was a food stand where we could have our lunch of soup, a hamburger, a glass of milk and maybe a candy bar if we skipped one item when I didn't bring my lunch. Very soon lunch pails were no longer needed for we had a new cafeteria serving good nutritional food choices by Mrs. Rebert, the head cook, assisted by the high school Home Education department in the 1939 centralized school.

Competition with other larger high schools bands was a challenge and we would be rated on the top-performing list most of the time. Many times we received the A+ ratings. My whole family including my grandchildren all was trained to play musical instruments. What an experience to be able to read music, it made a lifetime full of happiness appreciating the challenge it demanded.

In 1937 my first music teacher was a man named Charley Barone. He was born in Sicily and must have had a very natural and good foundation of musical training. His sons were all very musical as well. His oldest son Tony took over as director and instructor of our school band from his retired father and soon joined Herbert Ludwig instructing both the Barker and Wilson school bands, expanding their talents. The younger son Tommy played the trumpet and knew how to repair the instruments. Another brother Jimmy was a saxophone instructor and gave music lessons on the reeds. Old Charley was such a great man, I can still benefit from his influence when I hear the Sousa marches being played at the July 4th celebrations.

Our school Principal Mr. Pratt liked us to be the best by hiring the other fine talented instructor and added assistant director Herbert Ludwig. He was a former musician who played in the trumpet section under Director Arthur Fiedler of the famous Boston Philharmonic Pops Orchestra at that time. Tony and Herb worked together to kept up our fine ratings in the 1940's. When Tony was direct the director, he had me switch instruments from playing the trumpet to the euphonium (baritone). He ordered the treble clef version of the bass clef music so I didn't have to transpose the notes making it much easier for me to give my best for what he wanted in certain passages that this instrument required. I had to give my part with the baritone to excel at the appropriate moment, what a responsive thrill!

It was this instruction that lived with me the rest of my life for appreciating the composer's thoughts that put the feelings transferring into mine that stayed planted. When I hear music played with the right expressions it gives me the same thrill. Teachers that have this ability in any curriculum are to be praised. I was chosen 1942 or 1943 to go to All-State Teachers Convention at Syracuse to represent our school as a Euphonium player under the directorship of Craig McHenry of Ithaca College. I remember when I first joined the band playing the trumpet we went to Houghton College and had Edwin Franco Goldman direct us in an open pavilion, he was somebody special.

When I hear music it is overwhelming to have this brought back from the teaching at our little central school of these generous patient instructors that were paid very little money-wise but paid with the satisfaction of the results. I keep praising the school principal Milford Pratt of his understanding this quality and did everything he could to help promote the students to do their best. In 1937 he even convinced the school administrative board to treat the band students to a bus trip to the Shea's Theater in Buffalo to see and hear one of the famous bands at that time, the Paul Whitman Orchestra. For the satisfaction of excellence we produced at the competing levels that made us want to do all we could to out-perform even the largest schools in the State. What an added education this turned out to be later in my life. Teachers we have today at our school are giving their students this exquisite background for their future. God bless them for it is a "Time to Live."

CHAPTER 24
My Mother's Influence

My mother was a city girl who came to the country to marry my father. She learned a lot about country cooking by going to the Home Bureau, Ladies Aid meetings and working with the older ladies at church suppers. She always cooked and fed the men as well as the hobos noon meals and she had learned to have some of the best-cooked food in the country. Homemade bread, pies, taffy tarts all cooked on the wood burning stove.

One of my chores was to keep the wood box full at all times. It must have been something else for her to get a large meal not to have a refrigerator to store the food. Everything to be cooked came from home canned or fresh foods. Our neighbor had an icebox but that was quite a bother because they had to go five miles to the Lyndonville Cold Storage to get a 100# block of ice, and it lasted a few days. We had cows so we had fresh milk every day and it would spoil if kept overnight in the summer, so the icebox was a great help for those with no cows, they could keep it much longer in their ice box.

The 4.5% Guernsey milk always settled to the bottom and the cream to the top so whipped cream mixed with pure granulated cane sugar was a great treat with mixed dates, nuts and fruit, Jell-O's or chocolate and butterscotch pies, homogenized or pasteurized milk wasn't available yet. The cane sugar was purchased in a large fifty-pound sack and stored in the upstairs hallway of our house to keep dry. Homemade molasses cookies always with a dark raisin placed on center were delicious. The Germans did theirs a little differently, so any chance I had I would run over to play with my friend Paul Heidemann so I'd have a cookie treat. He would come back to our house for a cookie treat at our place too.

Mother's main hobbies were in the music field. She was trained at her school in the Canandaigua School to play the violin.

She taught herself to play the piano and could transpose music to a different key for a higher or lower purpose. I don't know how she did it by changing sharps to flats. When she married my father she soon became the church pianist after I was born.

Music was a common event in the homestead because a local friend, Gilbert Quigley, referred to as "Quig" a retired professional Irish singer with the greatest tenor voice I have ever heard from New York City who I think was as good as the famous Caruso. Quig told us that Caruso could break a glass beaker with his vibrating voice. I heard Caruso from a recording on the Victrola player for comparison. In the late 1890's and early 1900's the wind-up phonograph RCA Victrola 78 RPM's with a sound vibration needle and megaphone played these from the large recorded disks that were still around in homes in my early days. He gave us many of the albums we still can play today on the small crank disk recorder I purchased at an auction. What a treat to listen to this talent from the past! I can remember heating an old disk and shaping as a flower vase for a present to my mother for Mother's Day in the early 1930's at the country school.

My mother accompanied Quig for a number of years, singing in different churches all over our area as well as being in our own church choir. The music rehearsals in our home were beyond description. We had a lot of young people all about the same age and could they sing we made up a great harmonizing group. All could read music and sing their given parts. With Quig's professional training it gave us the definable proper breathing and voice presentations. Yes, with this training it gave us a real great feeling the rest of our lives when we hear songs sung this way. I call it super entertainment and to this day in 2013, one fine lady that was in our 1950 church choir was Marge Manley Perry now the church pianist having the talent playing the music with expressiveness to our church congregation for many decades. She still carries on with the expressions from the masters who gave us this kind of quality music. Quig and his wife Iva lived next to Marge's home in Millers, a small village of about 15 to 20 families about a half-mile south of the farm.

My mother wanted my brother and myself to be in the band at the Barker High School so we left the country school and took music lessons at a dollar each from director Charles Barone then Herbert Ludwig was hired who also taught us. What a plus this was in my entire life to be able to read music, sing the bass part, and play the trumpet and baritone. This pleasure also rubbed off to my children and grandchildren and has added much pleasure to our family lives when we assemble on the special occasions. I enjoyed singing either bass or baritone with the Niagara Orleans Barbershoppers Group for years.

In a 1936-37 building a new Centralized School System was offered by State assistance that a former alumnus of the country school became the Barker High School Principal. Milford Pratt, a very small man with energized leadership and talent, saw the advantage and influenced to the community and the school board to centralize. His father Harry Pratt being a County Line school trustee must have given him the insight and will to help others through this additional educational progress.

In 1939 his vision became a reality working with an official school board that were convinced it will enhance our community by the purchasing at that time two large farms for sports, recreation areas and the beautiful building of the well-planned addition with the still sparkling hallways to accommodate the state of the art facilities for the students, making this addition to the 1911 original building. I benefited using all the activities I could muster in; one was being a member in the first musical operetta "When Pa Was Courtin' Ma" on the new 1939 stage that has been used for performances over seventy years.

The only stage in the 1911 school was the gym and that was

used for everything, sports, band practices, concerts, singing and plays etc. When there was a play to be performed white sheets were strung up for the curtains. What an opportunity still with more of the progressive add-ons they are prepared to offer those to further their well-rounded education skills. I graduated in 1943 and in 2013 it will be seventy years ago.

During World War II my brother was in the Navy band playing the bass horn and also the string bass in the orchestra keeping the morale high on the troopships entertaining our soldiers back and forth across the oceans around the world, mother's wish came true.

Is this the Americana? In my opinion, I think so.

CHAPTER 25
German Traditions

The German men in the area would go once a year to a local woods, like a secluded place for privacy, and have a good old German- language-speaking party. I went once with my friend and played games and drank soda pop. The grownups had a little stronger brew. They were hard working people having a good time. My German friend Paul Heidemann's father had a sawmill and thrashing business. The machines they ran were always in excellent running condition. They also had a smoke house that was fed by burning hickory sawdust, which made the most delicious flavored hams and bacon that could be stored for a long time. Our German hired man cured meats we butchered with the same skill. They were hung in our cellar and during the winter then made good eating along with a casserole of baked beans and a heaping table spoon full many times and gone by springtime.

Paul loved to hitch up our horses and drive them on one of the spike tooth drags to help fit the ground in the garden. My father let him have this opportunity because they were such good neighbors and a good friend of mine we played together a lot. I loved to drive them too and many times took loads of apples to the canning factory. There was a certain amount of skill to control and handle their large bodies full of strength. We never had to whip them. They always stretched their muscles and gave all they could to respond to our commands. What a team!

One of my classmates in the rural school in the early 1930's was a daughter of the German Lutheran Minister named Helen Hein. I rode my bicycle down to their place and he was making the old fashion German sauerkraut. I had never sampled this kind of preparation before it had been fermented into the final taste. It was the fresh cabbage with the German touch that never left my memory. The right amount of salt, sugar and added vinegar was the secret formula that my folks didn't have. I guess when I go out for lunch many times I order a Rueben sandwich that seems to ring a bell in my memories thinking about that experience.

The Germans were proud of their days work; the old German hired man had this in his blood to do as much work as any man if  he got a little praise. When we had the hobos picking apples he tried to pick as many bushels as they did and got his dander into trouble. He was behind in the number of bushels the hobos had picked so after dinner he skipped his short rest period and came back to pick more to catch up. With a short rest, I went out in the orchard and found him hanging upside down with a bag full of apples. His foot had been caught between a limb and one of the ladder rounds. He was about two feet off the ground foaming at the mouth. I knew if I went for help he might not have made it so I pulled the ladder out to unfasten his locked foot and down he came headfirst. Within a few minutes he was back up the ladder having that built in urge to give all the energy he had to catch up. His pride was so strong to do his best, his will never ceased.

During World War II 1941-45 the farm was in full production like all the farms around. I wanted to mention that when I took a load of apples to Lyndonville, German War prisoners unloaded my wagon. A guard was around so they didn't try to escape. They appeared to be fine young men. Prisoners were kept in compounds fenced in with barbwire at night. We lived in a heavily populated German area but they were true Americans and except for a very few. You could trust their loyalty as good as any one. Many of their sons went off to war with the rest of the boys and just like the rest of us, some never came home.

CHAPTER 26
The 4-H Club Band

During this time mother (Ruth) and Grandpa Orson worked very hard to show the advantages offered by giving the country school students an opportunity to have a better education. They went to Holland, NY to see one of the first central schools.

Soon the country schools were closed and instead of walking a mile through snowdrifts, we were bused to the centralized schools at Barker and Lyndonville for the higher academic offerings; now there were many teachers each teaching not four grades but one of maybe three or four classes of the same grade. Ralph Weeks owner of the Ridge Road Express at Jeddo in 1937 started busing students to and from Barker High School. In 1939 our country school was closed.

With the Central Schools, many local students joined the band, and there were so many in fact, our local 4-H club formed a band. My mother Ruth organized and directed the 4-H band called "The Jolly Millers" in 1938-40. Here were our members that I can remember: Art and I Gordon Porter, Floyd Fisher, Clayton Corser, Larry Gotts, Jerry Yaxley, Laverne Hare, Wendell Johnson, Morris Smith, Van Powley, George Haight, Roger Foote, Betty Leonard, Gordon Gardner, Virginia Vickers, Dick Nellist and some others.

John Stookey, the Niagara County 4-H Agent, was a great help to promote us. We played all over, and even we were bused to Ithaca to play for the National 4-H Convention held at Cornell University.

127

1938 Jolly Millers Band in parade - 1938 - Lockport Fair
Ruth Porter conducting

The principal, Milford Pratt of the 1911 Barker School, was an alumnus from our country school and was very smart. He skipped grades and graduated from college very young. He found ways to get things he wanted for us to have a better education, like machine shops, aircraft instruction, a landing strip, school fairs and new additions, a beautiful auditorium to put on plays, band concerts etc. All were state approved and the cost to the taxpayers was reasonably accepted. The school let us use the old music band books and was on loan from the high school in Barker before it centralized.

Despite his small size, Mr. Pratt could take on the biggest student and put him in his place. In our area he informed neighbors about the advantages of centralizing the country schools. He had a stuttering problem but talked real slowly and you could hardly tell it was a problem. Talking slowly had an advantage for the older hard of hearing to understand all his proposals that made our school competitive with the city schools.

When my wife Nancy taught kindergarten at the central school 1951-52, still principal he observed her and would enter her room without her knowing it and he would be leaving when she looked up. Mr. Pratt wanted to keep tabs on a new teacher and make sure she was up to his standards, and she was.

CHAPTER 27
Boy Scouts in the 1940's

Offering a change in the community, there were a number of boys in the area in the early 1940's who had time on their hands, so the Lutheran and Methodist and other local men decided it was about time to give them something to do. We formed Boy Scout Troop #24. We met at the churches, but the idea of having our own building was soon considered. We decided to build a log cabin and the tax-free vacant property where the Methodist Church at Millers once stood was ideal.

Many of the local farmers were asked to donate trees from their woods. None refused, and soon we had enough to build a 20 x 30 foot log cabin with a huge fireplace. My brother Art got up a string orchestra to raise some money. By passing the hat through the crowd at the site, we were under way financially for building the log cabin for the scouts. I was one of the Scoutmasters along with Wilbur Lartz and Bob Nellist when he came home from World War II service was a great help in teaching the survival methods. I was talking to Dick Nellist and he said he was my assistant scoutmaster before he went into U.S. Army service.

We worked together and laid the cabin foundation. My father let me take the pick-up truck for the Monday night meetings. Some scouts lived a few miles away and had to be taken home later. They all had a way of getting there. We had wonderful people in the community helping us by saving their waste papers for raising money and helping with the war effort. James Watts, the grocery store owner, was nearby and gave us his support. Dad let me take the truck to Boy Scout Camp at Allegany State Park for a week. Each year two other parents helped out with the transportation. Some of the scouts were:

Richard Hare, Bob and Chester Chaffee, Stanley MacDonald, Bill Porter, John, Mark, and Gerry Haight, Roger Harrison, David Trinder, Ellis Thiel, David Thiel, Perry Chambers, Wendell Mears, John Riordan, William and David Walker, Dick Nellist and a few more.

Lyman Bigford became Scoutmaster later. Our cabin is not used for Boy Scouts anymore the cabin was finally move into secluded large wooded area off the Yates Center road and is used still by a private homeowner.

CHAPTER 28
A Boy Scoutmaster

Belonging to the Scouts had opportunities to do the activities that the city Scouts did such as going to the Boy Scout Camp at Allegany State Park near Salamanca.

I was single, available, and being the Scoutmaster for Troop #24 with the suggestion of my father and his permission to use the old used pick-up truck, we took the troop and supplies to camp for one week. At the camp we cooked our own food for two meals, raw bottled milk was available in the icehouse, the raccoons very cleverly opened the door took out the quart plugs and scooped out the cream that rose to the top of the glass bottles. What animals they were to figure that one out! The camp cooks fed us good evening meals and presented awards. There were the regular crafts taught daily and a compass lay out of hiking through the mountains to Thunder Rock or Big Basin maybe a five-mile journey under cover of the virgin forest.

The boys were anxious to go mountain climbing. It was something I had never done before. A very exciting challenge with the dangers that could occur, but we set out the northeast course from the camp that would take us to the path up another mountain to the huge rocks. As we started out topping the first mountain some of us found a good sturdy stick to carry, the first thing I could see wasn't a good idea. The boys had a strong urge to push over the dead saplings about the thickness of a baseball bat in diameter. One broke in half and fell very close to one of the boys. This was alarming to me he could have been knocked out or even bleeding. Knowing we were quite a ways from the camp and just as far from the path we were headed for, there was no way you could run back quickly for help. Firmly I said this was enough of being an Atlas Strong Man. They were a great group of boys innocent from any selfishness, very cooperative and respectable young men.

As we followed the compass direction and canteens of drinking water we came across a beaver dam with cotton-wood trees downed used in constructing a strong reinforced sealed structured dam by their gnawing and plugging the leaks for the little lake they had developed in a ravine. They gave us a flap or two with their tail in the backed up water to let us know for us to stay away. We disturbed the deer that were resting, getting up now and then by our intrusions. Finally, the compass proved fairly accurate and on the worn path up to the Thunder Rocks there was a welcomed fresh cool water spring that quenched our thirst that gave us a boost. A little later it started to rain and the camp sent a bus for a ride back. This was an adventure for me as well as the boys to see and climb up on the rocks hearing an echo of our voices as many young men had done previously. It also taught all of us the compass was a very important instrument to have along when hiking. In the evening we went with Dad's pickup truck with the headlights on to the camp dump and spotted the bears feasting on the leftovers.

Challenging games and just a lot of fun kept us from being homesick for the lake plains we were from. Hiking in the mountains was and always will be an adventure for father and son to learn about and know each other in a much different survival way than at home.

Our wonderful country and nearby Canada are full of all kinds of these boating, hiking, overnight camping places. Finding out that we humans taste good to the mosquitoes remind us and appreciate the conveniences we have at home. Finding a little odd stone or relic brought home is a reminder from those adventurous places that have now become memories to talk about during the short time we are given to live.

Being a scoutmaster was an adventure full of memories. I was glad to have had the opportunity to be able to lead our young friends in the local community. All turned out to be good citizens and many served our country when they were called upon to defend it. This also taught me when I had two sons I took time to take them into the wilderness for a very short boating, fishing and camping adventure. We are so used to being served by mother's cooking away from it lets you realize the value of her service at home.

This kind of fellowship is a rare privilege. I hope you haven't missed this experience.

CHAPTER 29
Century Farm Award

Our farm was located near Lake Ontario and about thirty miles east of the Niagara River. It was strictly a country living in our area. Most of the farms produce a mixture of fruit, dairy and grain products. Apples were the main fruit for commercial purposes. Bushels of apples were sent to the fresh market, many tons of apples were processed into applesauce the rest was pressed for making apple vinegar at the factories in Lyndonville, New York. There was an apple-drying evaporator close by those cored and sliced apples to be dried and shipped to the pie making factories.

Most farms in the 1940's grew vegetables such as cabbage, tomatoes, potatoes, sweet corn, melons, squash and small fruits. Chickens, hogs, some turkeys, ducks, geese and I guess about everything for a complete Sunday dinner. Many of the country boys could earn a little income like picking up the fallen apples or picking sour cherries.

Our farm received the Century Farm Award given to us by Governor Nelson and   Happy Rockefeller in 1968. Picture shows

brother Art and Mary, Ruth and Burton and Nancy and Gordon Porter.

My brother Art continued the fruit operation but larger farms could out-produce ours and so he became a part time farmer while working at Fisher Price Toys in Medina. When he died in 1990, his wife Mary could no longer operate the farm and other family members knew they couldn't make a living on the farm to support a family. The farmland was good enough to have the families fed to survive and keep the generations to take over where the older ones had left off. Now all that is left has to be written down as memories of hard work and happy lives. The family appreciated the privilege to be presented this commemorating plaque.

Mary eventually sold most of the land except the two houses, barn, outbuildings, a the good well, and about 10 acres of land that she kept. The land was purchased by Atwater Farms a local large dairy operation and now the orchards have become a big hay or cornfield.

Currently, the old 1826 farmhouse is being rejuvenated as living quarters, adding studs to the old plank house to insulate and modernizing the insides to the present day of living. It still has the hand hued beams and oak pegs and wide hardwood planked rooms that are exposed showing how it was so long ago. It took piles of wood in the winter to warm the cold winds that came through the cracks. The revealed open fireplace still has the iron sway bar with an S hook for cooking. There was plenty of wood to burn and with some muscle actions provided a comfort or discomfort we don't get today. The hot wood stove for cooking in the summer was almost unbearable for the women to cook meals for the men and hired help and stoking the furnace with split beach and apple wood chunks in the winter was an experience never to be forgotten mentally. It's so easy to turn up the thermostat as winter approaches now.

CHAPTER 30
Fruit Control

The old-two horse drawn spray rig was a one cylinder engine that could pump 200 to 300 pound pressure made by the Friend Company in Gasport, NY. It would take considerable time to cover all the orchards. Lime and sulfur, nicotine, and lead arsenate were the favorite sprays. Nicotine almost finished me. No masks for our protection we inhaled the powders. Occasionally the rig was used to put out threatening grass fires.

In the 1930's Dad was on top of the rig sprayed with his 4-nozzle boom and I sprayed the limbs underneath. Bugs were cagey critters, codling moth made wormy apples and were hard to control until our favorite spray DDT became available. It worked well, too well. No more codling moth, but it also affected the food chain interrupting the bird breeding cycles all over the continent.

I remember one farmer fed his cows some sweet corn stalks that had DDT sprayed on it to kill the bore. His milk was condemned and was dumped on the farm rock pile. Also the meat had to be destroyed it put him out of business. When we used DDT they said at the extension meetings you could soak in it without harm. I did get soaked under those trees but was lucky to wash it off with no harm.

As we used DDT, the red-banded leaf roller came along and laid a leaf over the apple, got underneath and ate away ruining some of the apples; they survived the DDT somehow out witting us humans and the scientist. Farmers are constantly battling one form of the problem or whatever crop or animals they are involved in. Then came the Friend Sprayer Company speed sprayers with 600 to 1000 pounds of pressure, and then came the concentrate sprayers.

By that time I was off the farm, my brother took over the fruit business. He had close calls with the deadly sprays like Parathion. One drop on his skin would affect his nervous system and his wife Mary had to rush him to the hospital in Medina for an antidote. Hazards on the farm were always present. Pictured is my brother, Art Porter showing me his brother Gordon with the proud apple crop.

Art died of cancer in 1990, maybe not related to the sprays, or breathing the tractor diesel fumes, but we wonder. The horses were long gone early 1950's at this time, otherwise they wouldn't have had a chance to survive such deadly poisons. Farmers use what the chemical industries sell them for controlling pests and still today many aren't the safest environmental solutions. The new chemicals are deadly but evaporate quickly after their purpose is done, so are of no danger. The whole new method of the fruit farming has changed so much in my lifetime. Most of the fruit can be picked without a ladder. I can remember the thirty-foot ladders stored in the back shed; my friends and I used to go hand over hand on the rounds above where our feet couldn't touch the ground but close enough so if we fell it wasn't a threat to be injured on the dirt floor. The thirty-foot Baldwin apple trees were huge apple trees that these ladders had to be used to pick the loaded fruit. There was a great demand for these varieties to make vinegar for preserving all kinds of fruits and vegetables. I still love the pickled Harvard beets, Seckel pears with a clove stuck in, and cucumbers that keep fresh in glass jars for a year or two. There were evaporators in every fruit community pressing and processing the juices to make the barrels of vinegar. Grandpa always had a large barrel of vinegar down cellar and now I have a little cute glass pitcher with a glass cork I use maybe sparingly a pint each year.

CHAPTER 31
Grafting Fruit Trees

Mice were a problem in the orchards for if their food supply was scarce in the winter they would girdle around the base of the trees for their survival food of a hard winter. So another early spring chore was to bridge graft the trees to keep them alive.

Grafting was a fascinating project. For bridge grafting, in the center of the tree we trimmed out the sapsucker limb shoots that grew straight up. We cut them to make about a foot long bridge depending on how high up the girdling was, dig down to the root and with a knife make a slit and place one end under the bark to the cambium layer matching the sucker shoot for nature to do its task with the contact and nailed to secure it then up above the girdled area caused by rabbits or mice. Another slit was made into the above bark with the same procedures, shoving the other end of the shoot into the slit and nailing making sure it was arched, so as the tree grew it wouldn't pull away from the graft, covering both ends with warmed bees wax. Once this was done, it was up to the Almighty to do the rest.

In the spring this amazing task proved successful and nature made the speedy healing recovery and saved the trees from sure death. Luckily this happened only a few times. Mouse bait was used by cutting up last fall apples in slices and treating with poison, putting the slices in the mouse run (paths) under the trees in the orchards. Now the ground around the trees is sprayed with grass killer and no more mouse runs. This affects the food supply for the birds that depend on their prey for their hatch out families.

Another grafting project was to graft different varieties of apples for better pollinating. This would give us more fruit with the help of busy bees. How we did this was to cut a budded sap sucker shoot called a scion about a half inch in diameter and four inches long taken from another selected variety tree making one end a wedge. We then had to cut off a main branch of the tree we were to graft, splitting the stub partly in the middle for an opening. Place this budded scion shoot into this slot having the sap layers meet, put warm bees wax around it to seal out the air so the surrogate tree could be changed to any variety we selected. This was another interesting project to check on to see how nature has a way we can manipulate for our benefit. Pitted fruits I had no experience doing. On the farm there was an old sweet chestnut tree that withstood the 1925 blight that destroyed most of the sweet chestnut trees and this one kept sending up shoots each year. I can remember my father saying how good the chestnuts tasted.

I had planted a Chinese Sweet Chestnut tree in my front yard so I grafted one limb with the original sweet chestnut scion and did get a crop of nuts. The only thing about doing this was a complaint from my wife Nancy was that the blossom smell came around the July Fourth when we had our family reunions and the musky smell was unpleasant. I agreed. In the fall it was decided that the tree had to go so I called Jake the tree remover to end the unpleasant specimen. He cut the tree down and ground up the roots I did get a taste of the nuts that came out of their spiny shells and enjoyed the project a few years of success I had done.

There are so many things on the farm that gave me the inner pleasures. God provides for you if you care to be patient to see the transition through. I suppose the doctors get this feeling when they can see the progress of healing the sick or fixing a wound. They are constantly asked to use their way of making a better life for those who need the help. Nowadays so many older people have joints like the knees or hips that become very painful and in no time have an artificial replacement in a few weeks gives that person a completely different attitude on life with such a cure. Some technical form of grafting can be applied to most anything with the right procedures for us to have; it's given to us His way of improvising a Time to Live.

CHAPTER 32
Apple Farm Duties

Our farm had a little less than one hundred acres. It was much larger at first but with hard times some acreage was sold to pay the taxes. After the Civil War, a son that took over the farm decided to take the advantage of homesteading going on in Wyoming. With a covered wagon, he took his family and left for an area for the west. This left my great grandfather to buy and manage the farm. The uncertainty of the cash crops making enough profit was hardly a break-even enterprise. After I had read the saved notes from my great grandfather, it was interesting to understand there was a labor problem. His son Orson had already graduated from the Yates Academy about 1887 and left the farm to work for his uncle in Rochester, Minnesota. One note said, " … if you don't return home we may lose the farm." This influenced Orson to return to the farm homestead, manage with his greater ability, to find a profitable venture to manage the land use, and to pay the taxes.

When the railroad came through Millers near Washington's birthday February 22, 1876 only a half-mile away from the homestead, it opened up a way to send the farm products to the large cities. In a few more years it became a very active railroad in this fruit belt area. The demand for Concord grapes was a profitable product so some of the acreage was planted with the grape vines and soon it paid off by shipping the harvested grapes to the city markets. If you went back to Millers Depot you would see the grape boxes piled in the foreground that held the grape baskets for shipping, I also remember the telegraph that used the Morse Code to communicate where the train was at that particular moment when my friend and I were inside visiting the clerk on our bikes.

The photos of the women grape pickers were a reminder of

that phase but soon competition by other farmers changed and the demand for apple vinegar became more profitable so half of the acreage was planted to a variety of apples. The grape packing house became a chicken coop for producing a little income from the sale of eggs and chicken meat.

I can remember the evaporators for making vinegar and the dry houses with its furnaces burning soft coal for drying apples. Eating a slice of the freshly dried apple was a treat I'll never forget. It became a demanding product in the apple pie industry; some dried apples were even sent overseas. The apples were at their peak around Halloween time and fresh cider became a real treat for the parties that they gave the young ones to meet and play all kinds of games in the church basement. Bean bag relays passing the bags under then over to the next one in back and then the back one would run up to be in front to start over the course again. By the time we went through all the line the first one that started ended back up to the head of the line, the first group to do it was the winner. There were teams to challenge each other so the room was sure buzzing. Trick games added to the fun but sometimes it wasn't funny for the one that was tricked.

Another game I can think of we did was by placing apples to float in a tub almost full of water and with no hands only biting the apple or the stem to raise the apple out of the tub with your mouth became a real challenge and some apples were hung from a string to get with your hands behind you. This was always a lot of fun to participate or watch. After the games for refreshments the older ladies gave us homemade fried cakes and fresh cool cider. These annual parties we looked forward to having as soon as the month of October was turned up on the calendar.

Apple varieties kept improving through the Extension Service Experimental Station at Geneva, New York. There was an annual Fruit Show held in Rochester for the fruit farmers to attend and see what has been developed through the year presenting the newest of varieties and equipment. It was a thrill to attend and see what new ideas were available offered by the Experimental Station. One of the old varieties of apples was called the Wolf River apple. It was a huge apple about six inches in diameter but had very little flavor when I tasted once and it soon disappeared from the orchards its size also created a processing problem.

Today the varieties are grafted to dwarf stocks many can be picked without a ladder; this helped to prevent a lawsuit from injuries falling from such heights. The names of some of the varieties are still around like MacIntosh, Delicious (that has a butt end like a sheep nose), Cortland that when peeled, the under layer stays white much longer than any of the other varieties. I loved the Waldorf Salads of this variety made with these apple diced slices, English walnuts, either dark or white raisins, and salad dressing. This adds to a meal especially on the Thanksgiving Day celebration.

CHAPTER 33
Dangerous Bulls

If you have ever watched or have been to a Rodeo or have seen an experienced a Toreador in a bullfighting ring it gives you some idea how a bull changes his mind that can produce a widow. There are plenty of men some dressed as clowns to distract them. On the farm the clowns aren't around so the dangers are always present with these up to two thousand pound animals. When there was a breeding of a cow I had been hired to perform, I had this experience. Luckily he did his duty and behaved, all precautions were taken.

My father gave me a calf to be raised for a 4-H project so I turned the rabbit pen into a calf stall. She was a Registered Guernsey and she was a great lot of fun to be around.

My mother forbid having a bull on the farm and my female (heifer) at sixteen months of age it was time for her to become a mother we had charts that showed the approximate weight by her heart girth, at 64 inches or about 760 pounds, it was time for me alone to lead her with a rope down the road two miles to a farm who had a Registered Guernsey bull to be mated for pregnancy. All the milking cows were taken to the bull for breeding after a two months waiting period to be ready for mating after they had calved. We had eight Registered Guernsey's, five we milked daily.

Today the sanitation is extremely guarded with the milk flowing through the sterilized stainless steel piping directly to be cooled so the bacteria is much better controlled. Pasteurization kills the good as well as the other bacteria that may be prevalent. Being brought up as well as our customers who purchased our raw milk products for years may have benefited by the good it had, maybe it should be investigated further. The pills that are consumed now are not all giving the protection needed. This is only a thought I have, again it is not a cure but to have an open mind of how nature and the Almighty has given us the curiosity there is time to examine all possibilities.

Within a year or two this animal was one to be selected to inseminate by the new service offered by the veterinarian. What a relief to eliminate one more of the dangers and hazards that were always prevalent connected to the advancement of the way we lived. We had to be a member of the New York Artificial Breeding Cooperative Inc. with the influence by the Cornell University and the Extension Service to provide the necessary information given to the elected farmers to maintain the new-formed business of

artificial insemination. As the conception improved it was a fast growing service that became time consuming for the vets. This service was then handed over to a special layman employee to handle and provide this service who could perform without a College Degree in Animal Husbandry. In 1940 this receipt was sort of another Twentieth Century historical event that happened across the country at this time. It was hard to believe but my mother had one less worry of becoming a widow.

We had to be a member of the New York Artificial Breeding Cooperative Inc. A refundable registration fee of $5.00 plus a one-time $1.00 assessment for the ten cows using the service, like many farmers we welcomed the convenience.

Dairyman: Burton Porter
Address: Barker
Cow E.T. (Ear Tag) No. 1937

Reg. No. 383422
Date. 12/24/40

Time of insemination: 3 P.M.

Sample from Bull
    Name: Renown
    Registered number 216597
Number of Service: 1st
Method of Insemination

Remarks: 8 years old 5 hours
           (noticed heat or estrus before service)
Treatment: Buttercup Porter -Kin
Receipt for the service: $5.00
Veterinarian: Dr. G. M. Badger

In our farm records I found this receipt dated near the beginning of the A.I. service 12/24/1940 (I added from the abbreviations to understand the information)

This welcomed service became available soon after the program was developed in the USA. and in New York State by the Department of Animal Husbandry at Cornell University Ithaca, New York.

This 1940 receipt I noticed the Dr. marked down for "Remarks" the timing of when we noticed our eight year old was cow in estrus (5 hours in heat) shown keeping it for further Laboratory Research someday. This was the beginning of keeping the records before the historic huge Cornell Computer that filled a large room was used to store the essential build-up of the additional genetic traits and records obviously needed for the improvement that was realized for the milk production.

The farmers were anxious to obtain their better way of life with a larger monthly milk check if it could be done with the added records for a more productive female.

Using artificial Insemination also replaced another farm hazard on the farm eliminating the dangerous unpredictable bull that cost much more to keep with very little reliable records for improving the herd by guess. Sometimes there was a chance that he could have been a great improver. Life expectancy is fairly short and not knowing with such few daughters was sent to the market before knowing his great genetic ability he may have had. Below is Father's receipt for the service. He paid cash for the insemination service.

CHAPTER 34
The Original A.I. Breeding Procedures

In 1947 on the farm in November the harvesting was about completed and my brother Art came home from the Navy and married in May. There were now three of us to run the small farm. The acreage wasn't large enough to support all of us and at the time I was a single twenty-two year old and wasn't needed on the farm.

There was an Inseminating Training Course for Dairy cattle recently developed by the Professors at Cornell University that was offered. My father encouraged me to take it. In 1947 I took the course and in 1948 was on my way of becoming a manager. At that time training was by those Professors and it was an educational experience trained to be a technician manager. Professor Bob Spaulding a fraternal lodge brother I got acquainted with, rode with me to the training area in Cortland, NY. He was one of the professors who made sure we were using the correct artificial insemination procedures by showing us the specific area for the semen to be placed for the best results. Some of the trainees were sent home failing to be able to locate the proper area.

A.I. procedures started in 1938 and by 1940 we had our first cow inseminated by Veterinarian Dr. George Badger. As he kept expanding his doctoring, it was apparent his time was more valuable just being the animal doctor. Later Burton C. Hall a dairy farmer's son became the technician manager and in time built up the breeding business needing assistance. Soon with the increase customers, it became too much for one technician and the area was soon divided almost equally. I would estimate there were about between 10,000 to 12,000 female animals of breeding age in the county. We inseminated 7,000 of these each year for the Co-op member's herds and the competitive technicians had plenty to give them their stud's service also. A few farmers still used the natural method of owning a bull for convenience but unable to check daily for the estrus in younger animals breeding age.

Burt and I both were presented the National Association of Animal Breeders for the 100,000 Award for having accomplished 100,000 first services for meritorious service, and for outstanding leadership in livestock improvement. This became a lifetime occupation when he shared with me the privilege of covering the eastern half of Niagara County as manager technician. At the yearly annual meetings this farmer organization lead by the farmer members elected a Board of Directors of the Niagara County Artificial Breeding Co-op affiliated with the New York Artificial Breeders Cooperative Inc. I was a farmer Co-op member with my father. Working as a technician with Burt about six months as a relief Technician Inseminator throughout Niagara County being trained and ready was hired for the eastern half of Niagara County as manager.

I began meeting and providing the service for the friendliest, absolutely down to earth group of congenial people that anyone could be ask to serve. I can say upon retiring I missed them as much as anything except my own family.

When I started inseminating, nothing had changed from the original procedures for my first ten years. We used sterilized glass catheters and syringes and with rubber sleeves we washed with disinfectant each time. We had to wash the catheters with a solution, rinsed with distilled water and heated in a roaster oven at 250° for 15 minutes. The liquid semen extended with egg yolk was sent to us every day except Sunday by bus from Ithaca in a box shipped to the Lockport post office that had a balloon filled with water that was frozen and rapped with paper insulation placed in glass test tubes sealed with corks. This kept the liquid semen at a 40° an ideal temperature good for at least three days. There were a choice of two Holstein, one Guernsey, one Jersey, one Ayrshire, one Brown Swiss every day and one Angus beef bull semen was shipped three times a week for smaller calves. Going through a number of trials the first was the glass catheters and syringes that had to be washed with distilled water and sterilized each day.

It was a problem when one would break inside the animal to remove that far into the uterus and out through the cervix then the vagina. I had a couple break and probably other technicians did too, it wasn't the easiest location to get it out and removed. It was soon replaced by a throw away plastic catheter but being flexible was a little more effort to get the feeling for the right location. The glass syringes had to be washed the same way and a new little rubber hose reattached to the catheter was sort of makeshift. A plastic throw away sleeve replaced the rubber sleeve eliminating disinfecting after each insemination. Soon a little plastic throw away syringe that slipped on the plastic catheter was introduced that didn't satisfy most of us.

When I first started before the local coop divided the county I worked with manager technician Burt Hall who covered the whole county the supply semen was split and put into test tubes so I could cover the area nearest where I lived. Before starting on our calls we would go upstairs in the post office where the Farm Bureau office was located and checked the sperm count mortality rate under the microscope to make sure there was plenty of live sperm to do the job. This was done each day except Sundays and a double supply was sent on Saturday because the office was closed. If the semen was kept at 40° in a little ice filled box and would be useable for at least three days. This too also amazed me how the life of these microscopic cells can be so strong to take this kind of maneuvering.

We went through a number of experiments trying to be more efficient through the years. Experiments with frozen semen was tried and found that the egg yolk extender called glycerol added helped to keep the semen alive in the frozen stage. Dry Ice was used to freeze and store the semen, it was made available in glass vials for farmers who wanted special sires and would store much longer. In the 1960's I made an insulated box with a glass thermos container filled with Isopropyl Alcohol and Dry Ice with a rack to hold the stored frozen semen. This was not a good way to have because I had to use a file to scratch the stem then break open the little vial, when doing this one vial broke into pieces. I saved very little of the semen in a towel only a drop or two amazed by what little amount there was but the female became pregnant. It was make shift but worked. I bought the dry ice from the local druggist Joe Ruebel who received it from RICH'S, the ice cream deliverer; sometimes I had to go to the Union Carbide Co. in Niagara Falls for the dry ice.

As competition started in the area they came with nitrogen tanks with frozen semen. It wasn't long when the co-op could see we had to convert to this method of storage and soon they furnished us with the new nitrogen tanks filled with a choice of semen that was competitive to the others. There was a lot of experimenting with different catheters, the first was glass rods then plastic, and it was the same with the syringes. The glass vials were replaced by the French straws that were like a ball point refill filled with the frozen semen and a new type of catheter was put to use that held the straw in place with a throw away sheath to secure it during the insemination. Then we were introduced to a stainless steel plunger rod pushing the semen out a much easier stable mechanism and the whole process was unique and efficient. Once a month the supply truck was met for refills and nitrogen. This has been the procedure for over twenty years and in many cases some the farmers themselves bought themselves tanks and bred their own cows. We sold them the semen of their choice they selected. All these changes have produced outstanding productive animals for their herds to keep in business.

In the beginning offering the A. I. service many farmers who had one or more cows in their barns were ready to join and become members of the coop so we had many small customers. Still many of the larger farms had bulls for breeding their cows and heifers but always had to be on guard for the bull that would suddenly turn on them and either kill or permanently injure or scare the daylights out of them, the stories these farmers told me about close calls were real. So selling the convenience was fairly easy if we were able to get the cow pregnant (with calf). Having a local phone on the east side area the farmers started making their calls to me to save a fifteen-cent toll call. This expanded the eastern area to grow for service and soon it was too much for one technician and the service area was divided fairly close to halves. This gave me the eastern part of the county to manage full time. The local farmers controlled the co-op and elected officers set up an annual dinner meetings, this brought farmers together for the progress reports we presented and voted on who should be the best qualified farmers to run the business to pay the technicians the monthly salary based on the duplicate receipts with the money turned in to the elected farmer treasure paid us both our share of the service fees. There were many local co-ops affiliated with the central headquarters that were dairy farmers elected to see that the overall program worked efficiently and hired field managers to see that the business kept the technicians informed of the whole procedures worked to give the farmers the best service.

.   The men that were our field men and advisers kept close track by riding with us at an undisclosed time checking the accuracy of our records and encouraged us with praises. The farmers themselves were the biggest and most helpful of all, I can't say enough for those who work seven days a week to provide milk products and meat for us to buy for our families. Only they know what it's like to go to the barn and milk cows every day being healthy, not feeling good some days or like going to an auction not getting back in time for a milking. Many times the women or wives would fill in to keep the business rolling. It was a family operation that took years of experience to succeed.

Just before I retired in 1987 I had the opportunity to be involved with the process of freezing living embryos.

Veterinary Doctor collecting embryos

Artificial Inseminator – Gordon Porter

The Walter Van Buren Farms were connected with an Embryo Freezing Company I was called to inseminate a number of outstanding older cows I think over seventy that had very high records officially classified with strong type conformation bodies. The veterinarians who came with a van loaded with the intricate equipment for this purpose injected hormones into each cow to induce multiple eggs for me to fertilize with selected semen they provided, then I was called to inseminate each cow the two inseminations a day apart by placing the semen with these top selected proven sires. In two days these embryos were flushed out at the 8 to 16-cell stage, which was just before the development of the fetuses. Again the microscopes were used to search for the tiny living embryos. The veterinarian doctors were successful in securing a number of fertilized embryos for freezing with liquid nitrogen that would be kept then thawed and placed in surrogate cows around the world. I know that some were sent to Japan and other countries for their demand. It's amazing how these little creatures could be manipulated shoved around frozen stiff then thawed to produce a healthy living animal. To me it was just fascinating to be able to be a part in this situation on how life can be frozen to keep for many years.

This could have been the forerunner to aid the procedures as in the human family development that will be used more and more for those who are delaying the conception. They could have the fertilized embryo flushed out and frozen and saved waiting for in one reason or another; then a surrogate mother would be used to carry and give the birth at a more convenient time.

A new approach to this is space traveling. It would be so easy to transport the tiny frozen embryos carrying the accentual ones needed for the populating or food survival on another planet if there was and probably will be someday a way to have an artificial surrogate to mother it.

On the farm there were so many things we did to improve our way of "A Time to Live" that could apply and give us the urge to extend our thinking far beyond the possibilities for a better life. The scientist keeps advancing toward a certain goal for some reason by altering the genetic code.

CHAPTER 35
The Artificial Insemination Manager Techniques

Artificial Insemination fully developed in Denmark in 1938 and became a much safer way to eliminate the dangerous bull that had to be kept on the farm only for breeding purposes. He was unpredictable weighing up to two thousand pounds with his temper and had to have a ring put in his nose that seemed to dull his actions. A staff was hooked onto this ring providing the farmer a little space the only way to handle him when he had his only duty to perform. The bull stud at Ithaca, NY added all the safety precautions necessary for protecting the semen collecting staff.

It was a new growing industry that replaced the unruly farm bull and it fit my farm related education perfectly. I was familiar handling these bovine animals, and I owned a small herd with my father of the Registered Guernsey breed. When artificial breeding became available we had our first animal inseminated in 1940 by Dr. Badger our veterinarian, the procedures hadn't changed when I had the training.

On February 18, 1949 I was hired continuing daily inseminating service for thirty-eight years and was one of few honored in Columbus, Ohio by the "National Association of Artificial Breeders" for inseminating over one hundred thousand successful services when I retired August 1987.

I was selected to be the host for a Danish Farm Representative from Denmark who rode with me one day to see the breeding procedures in artificial insemination while making my daily calls. My mother then my wife Nancy relayed the calls to me. As time went on with the headquarters up on the hill at Ithaca, New York. The New York Artificial Breeders Co-op later changed its name to Eastern A.I that included a larger area and they installed a call answering service. I could push a button to get the recorded message from the farmer for the needed service this expanded even more a toll free operator for me to get my daily line-up route. I tried to be at each farm as close to a regular given time that worked best for my line up and for the farmers' convenience and be ready to have the animal confined for my service.

When using AI how does the cow feel not having a male? I'm sorry I can't answer that question. Cows in estrus are quite cooperative to artificial inseminate. The farmer placed his call to inseminate for his cows he wanted bred that was in estrus. Generally for the highest conception rate were the ones noticed in the early to midday morning and were inseminated in the afternoon. The ones with estrus in the afternoon were inseminated the next morning. This usually gave me a spread of a few hours to get the job done but when they showed Saturday after noon, Sunday was a must, so with a leeway I generally managed to join my family for Sunday worship but hastily changed clothes for my job.

The cow would menstruate about two days later. This didn't mean she didn't conceive but did show her correct very close to a regular twenty-one day cycle. If in three weeks she again menstruated, she in most cases was open (not with calf). She was then marked on the calendar to shorten a few anxious days given a hormone to start an estrus. The veterinarian was well trained to examine for this also checking pregnancies helping the farmer know if the conception occurred. Easter and Christmas were no service days but I still occasional calls for a high production animal that didn't conceive on more the three tries. Three more weeks waiting may shorten her chance of staying in the herd because eventually her production would suffer.

What are the signs of estrus? The cow is in a state of sexual excitability and the only time that she will accept a male and is capable of conceiving. At this stage she's a very much erotized animal letting out a bawling call and being mounted by other females. Some hardly show any outwardly signs and in some cases are given hormones by the veterinarian for her to be artificially inseminated to conceive. In the winter where some cows were confined in stations a farmer would lean over near the one marked down to watch and if she would show a sign of mounting even an urge with her head up to jump on the farmer it gave him a clue to place a call. This occurs every 21 days until pregnant. Breeding charts and date wheels are very closely watched near this time with her given ear tag number for it is important that she will become pregnant near the 60-90 days after she has given birth for the maximum profitable milk production cycle.

I had customers that had bought land to farm in my area from many different nationalities. Some were in the process of learning the English language. I think it's important to mention this because it really was historic to me to work with these people who came to try to survive like the rest of us.

The American Indians from the reservations called me with their own thoughts only they understand, yet they sent many of their sons to help defend and build this great nation. The English, Scotch in New England and the Irish around the coastal regions made up many of the first land purchasers that traded with the American Indians trading land for furs and needed tools. I was called to their farms for my services in artificial breeding.

Some customers worked in the factories here and made enough money to buy their own farmland with the desire to be more independent from the hot fire furnaces of the foundries or experts in the scientific fields. Some owned only one or two cows, but they would call me to service.

The Estonians had a pond dug on their property for a cold dip then to a shanty (Sauna) with heated stones to clean their pores. On one of my visits, my customer "Imar" proudly showed me his cleansing system. Dan was a big strong man from the Russian Ukraine. He had an interesting life seeking the freedom all came here to have and something they couldn't have abroad. The Swedes a very friendly group that expanded with a few cows into the area with different ways to make a living. The Italians gave it a try but many went back to the city to start delivering vegetable produce to the local grocery stores. The Hungarians were so pleasant and happy to have this privilege of owning their own farm. The Polish were very smart people and managed to stay and work as hard as they could to raise their families and give their children the education needed for the future. I made friends with a few Czechoslovakians too. The Canadians who came here were actually from other countries and had crossed the open borders to get away from the British rules of the monarchies. What an experience I had going into all the different homes of my customers to collect the fees for my service. Some revealed their experiences they had had abroad. It was a touch of their pride that I witnessed and could feel their whole-hardiness of being a partner in this great country. This first hand contact was such a pleasant understanding of how we all can get along. Who would ever have thought that in Niagara County, NY, so much of the "world" would have come to my doorstep?

Inseminating was an education of learning how life begins with its miraculous fertilization. In the bovine breed you are able as if being blindfolded to reach through the rectum with your arm wearing a throw away plastic sleeve glove and through a soft membrane grasping the cervix inside the vagina and with a stainless steel catheter covered with a sterilized sheath loaded with bull semen guide it through the small open channel into the uterus body in the most acceptable place near the division of the two uterus horns. The training at first was given under the guidance at the Animal Husbandry Division at the colleges by the professors. In 1947 I was fortunate to be accepted with some of the beginning trainees for this procedure. Living on the farm and knowing the natural and artificial way was a help to understand this new service.

Making a great number of healthy calves there were a number of twins and a few triplets. With twins if the results produced one male and one female the female was called a "free martin." In most cases, it was genetically understood that this cow would fail to have the sexual organs to produce and it was usually advised if raised, to be kept for veal or beef purposes only.

Raising the resulting offspring has been improved over the years from the way it had been done like we did in the past. Calves like comfort and cleanliness rather than confined and tied in a tight stall that is hard to clean. They like the freedom not being tied but having a little exercise in the outside calf pens in temporary little hutches which provide a great way to start these newborn females. You think it's not right to leave them out in the cold so young at a day or two old if kept in the barn sometimes ending up having pneumonia or scours. Out in the sunshine and the fresh air with good windbreaks, it has proven without a doubt the best way to raise a healthy female heifer calf. Also with all this fresh bedding they let you know they are happy. All domestic animals would respond this way if given a chance.

Now the latest information I have 2012 a new development of experimenting as of the beginning in the year 2002, is a method of inseminating cows with "Sexed Semen" that is 90% reliable. It was now available since 2008 for the dairy farmer to buy this semen for the mating that will give them only female offspring this sounds impossible. Talking to a farmer that has used this procedure, he indicated that he has purchased this semen with good results. It is expensive to purchase but placed in the best performing animals for mating could be a good investment. They have somehow eliminated the Y male sperm to obtain only female X sperm to be frozen and available for insemination. Nature's way usually produced close to 50/50 results females and males. I can't get over how the Almighty balances things like this and the initiative for those to bring about this is awesome. Changing nature's rules could eventually create more laws and problems of what we are supposed to abide by. God created the heaven and the earth. Some families have all boys and some have all girls but averages close to half and half. That's the way it was but with artificial insemination now there is a way to select.

I remembered the Fuehrer Adolph Hitler in 1945 WWII tried to develop a Master Race by selection. If he was here now he had the idea but to connect all the proper genes together would be a gigantic task, there are possibilities but it would take thousands of records to make it possible. Are you thinking what I am thinking?

With dairy cattle they have made this become a reality. I hope it will always be used for the benefit of man and not misused. I don't have the complete knowledge how the DNA works but it may become useful to get the results needed. It has been proven with the computer records what sires can be used to improve certain characteristics such as milk production and certain improved conformations through the sire selections that we started to develop when I was going from one farm to the next keeping and sending in the records.

I suppose as we began to use computers to store these desirable or not desirable characteristics that were predominate, some sires have produced some nervous disposition females. The technician and the farmer knows it can be dangerous to be kicked. Being kicked a few times myself, I preferred the gentle docile animal to inseminate. The farmer lets you know when he has one if she injured him while bending down twice daily in a vulnerable place where it could happen. On our farm in the 1930's milking by hand we had what they called "kickers" that hooked on the back of the joint above the hock of both legs with a short adjustable chain and when she raised her foot it kept her from knocking over the pail full or you off the milk stool. Of course now many are milked in milking parlors and if one acts up she may take a ride and end up on the meat counter.

Sometimes there is crisis and having the milk industry; milk becomes a reliable substantial available needed food. We must protect our dairy industry until there can be a better way for our security. I did have a few incidents when I first started as the inseminator that drew some respect for the animal I was to inseminate.

It was a single cow one farmer owned that had a two-month-old nursing calf in a box stall with a headlock. I would have had to put her in the headlock but being a complete stranger she looked at me as if I was going to take away her calf. Well, I got her chilling look message through her eyes and she meant it, I quickly got out safely till the farmer showed up.

In another case I remember the veterinarian had worked on the cow the day before and when I approached her she gave a spontaneous powerful kick that hit my right hip that spun me around throwing me against the wall. I carried a nose lead with me but failed to be able to use it by her head-strong determination. I left and made more calls to return when the farmer could help me to make sure I would have some help. There were some more through the thirty-eight years, but luckily never had any broken bones. This profession has certainly been a rewarding venture in my farm country life experience. Dangers will never cease in most any profession.

CHAPTER 36
Nature At Its Best

I had the opportunity to see nature at its best as I traveled seven days a week, approximately 40 to 45 thousand miles a year, for 38 working years. This added up to a conservative 1,500,000 miles around the eastern half of Niagara County. The town, county and state highways were at a point of improvement some from the original gravel with potholes that could put your front alignment to be realigned to the MacAdam Road building improvements that the State encouraged and recommended for the new foundations that gave a much better surface for safer driving.

Very seldom was I held up by this yearly construction that saved my windshields that were broken a few times by a stone thrown up by an approaching car or service truck. Sometimes the highwaymen helped me out of a snowdrift and sometimes I would help a school bus in need of a little assistance with my shovel. Spring flooding along the creek was a hazard and in the Prussia area, Gustav had to come with his high wheel tractor to carry me from the road through the knee deep flooded path with my case to his barn on a knoll for the waiting female for my service.

My daily service schedule kept me informed on most every farm that was on back roads about what was happening with this transformation. I became familiar with the phone company men who were working putting in new lines for private businesses like mine that depended on the faster services and the power company men working in all kinds of weather sometimes restoring power to the needed farms after a power shortage.

The four seasons in Niagara are spectacular. I bought a new or used car almost every year. There were many I traded for the best service and economy Fords, Chevrolets, Nashes, Volkswagens, Corvairs, Vegas, Mazdas, and Spectrums, over 30 altogether. In most cases it was an advantage to trade with the local car dealers yearly with their reasonable offers than to have a breakdown that could disable my services.

I observed migrating birds, turkey buzzards, pheasants, hawks, indigo buntings, orioles, scarlet tanagers, owls to name a few and deer, and the night prowling dead raccoons and opossums struck by autos on the highways in the middle of the night I had to dodge; providing food for the ugly looking buzzards to clean up. The season changes of spring greens to fall reds, oranges and beiges. Snow covered evergreens, iced limb wonderlands, frosty sparkles in the sunlight, just indescribable beauty. This was a 7-day a week venture with variable hours, but only once I couldn't make it home because of the weather. The 1977 snowstorm was the big one. I was snowed in for three days at the Royalton Center Store. Mrs. Gardner, a store customer, offered her home to three of us stranded men, so we were in a cozy well heated home during the wintry blast. Walking from the store to her house just about 500 feet away; it was a walk through huge drifts, I was dressed warm but the cold was very bitter in the zero temperature I felt I might freeze to death. My car was completely covered with a snowdrift. I still would take the snow in preference to the disastrous storms elsewhere.

The farmers had it much worse because they couldn't let up on the milking and had to dump the daily milking until the milk truck was able to get to their barns. The wind continued to howl and snow to pile up with no let up. Rotary snowplows were used to open up the highways after the wind ceased. Some houses were almost completely covered. A local boy shoveled my car out, I still feel bad not giving him a tip.

Once a month the district manager would bring us up to date on the latest bull proofs or procedures for better service. Being at the far end it was traveling up to one hundred and fifty extra miles round trip after a day's work of traveling, it was meeting with all the

Co-op technicians covering the counties in Western New York. We met at the best restaurants where they treated us with great meals that night. Once a year we would travel to Ithaca to the stud and business center for more information and always heard a professional speaker talking about how to hit the hot button with the public we worked for. They kept us awake and held our attention with stories and ways to satisfy our clients. The technician's wives were always welcomed, entertained and given a chance to meet including an opportunity in a short session to talk to each other about the woman's important role in carrying on the business.

CHAPTER 37
Learning To Start and Drive the Model T

I was given the responsibility to start the 1925 Ford Runabout that was my first experience with driving an automobile. Before, my father would let me sit on his lap and steer, so I learned from watching what he did.

On the steering wheel the left lever was to advance the spark to start the motor next to the radiator in front under the right

1925 FORD
MODEL T RUNABOUT

headlight was a simple little choke wire to pull that went to the carburetor, I had to pull and when it started after a few cranks with the handle in the front of the truck (being careful the way you positioned your hand in case it kicked

backward and could break your arm). You had to run around quick and push the left spark advance lever up to keep the motor running and from back firing. The right lever was like the gas pedal, way up would idle and down would give you more speed like the riding lawn mowers we have today. The button when pushed made the horn make an "a-ooga" sound. It wasn't used much because we hardly ever passed anyone; at that time, there were not many cars on the road. There was a hand brake to the left by the left knee that also was used for the cruising speed. The windshield wiper was hand operated, in a rainstorm he had to crank it back and forth, terrible in a snowstorm. It was all you could do to keep steering, working the hand levers and foot pedals and keep from running off the narrow roads. Dad let me drive it to the orchards when I was about twelve, I couldn't wait for the opportunity.

When we visited maybe once a year riding on the new Highway Route 104 in 1929 when Herbert Hoover was President to see someone with this Model T, probably cousins in Rochester or in Webster, NY. I can remember it was called the new million-dollar highway on the Ridge. The truck had a little boxed area in back could carry a few needed supplies like a couple of dozen newly made apple baskets to take to the orchard for the pickers. On the running board was a metal box holding the tools to change a flat tire or adjust the carburetor. It had side curtains to break the wind a little and the heater was a little hole in the floorboard that put in a little heat from the motor to keep our feet from freezing.

One winter my father was driving, my brother seated in the middle, and my mother held me on her lap. We were cold, but with a large wool horse blanket covering us and wearing the big homemade gloves made of dog skin was enough to help us be comfortable. It must have been Sunday or maybe Thanksgiving, Grandpa (Orson) must have done the chores. I was really glad to get back home to a warm house. This also gave us a ride to church or to visit local relatives and friends. Equipped with narrow wheels there were times of getting into a mud hole on the dirt roads so my brother would steer and push the forward foot pedal and my father would give a push in back to get us out. So when the new road was laid the change was welcomed.

Progress was, and is, an ongoing experience through these years that seemed very hard at the time. Even still, what changing times I've lived through; A Time to Live has been so eventful.

CHAPTER 38
Learning To Fly

I was always interested in flying, When the Italian Fleet with Balboa flew over our farm in 1933 on his way to the Chicago Century of Progress Fair, and I looked up and saw the Squadron of planes I think there were nine planes. Also about that time a huge Dirigible (Graf Zeppelin) that I saw flew over the farm on the Niagara-Orleans County Line. It was a big thrill for a farm boy to see something like this way out in the country. Living fairly close to Lake Ontario maybe they followed along the lakes for navigation.

In 1932 when I was about six or seven years old my father and uncle took me to Rochester and to the airport where the pilot let me climb into the cockpit to see the altitude   instruments of one of the planes. That really was special and from then on after I saved my money and took flying lessons at a small airport near Lockport. The lessons were $10.each. Louie, my instructor, taught me a few things about flying; it was that urge I wanted to experience never had flown before.

Louie taught me a full throttle for take-off was what would take us up and up. He showed me how the controls reacted. One hour of putting the plane into tail spins and maneuvering the controls back to the even flight, learning to land in an emergency, picking a good field to land in case the power was suddenly discontinued, were all topics he went over with me. Upon landing, he taught me a way to slide the plane at an angle to lower our flight to prevent overshooting the runway. After ten lessons my money ran out but I did handle the controls and could have soloed the two-seater Porterfield aircraft.

While watching the Canadian geese in the spring some in flight spotting a safe place to land would be higher up than the flock and by turning their bodies into a sliding maneuver they did the same effect Louie taught me included in the lessons. I did benefit doing this having the pleasure of watching our migrating friends the natural way most everyone never sees or knows the reasoning for such a drastic way for some to descend.

During WW II, not being drafted yet, I signed up to be an aircraft spotter located at the Brigham Farm on Burgess Road in the Town of Somerset. When we heard or spotted one we would go to the provided phone connected to a relay station give the proper flight direction if we had one to report. This was our defense that soon was replaced by the Radar Systems.

I was given a ride in a biplane that a city farmer owned near the lake. We took off on his make-shift runway toward the southwesterly wind but as soon as we took off a north lake breeze came up. When we came in for the landing to the southwest runway it took a lot of maneuvering to fight a north crosswind. We

dipped landing on one wheel almost flipping over in the open cockpit and ended up right side up thank goodness, into the cow pasture. This sort of cured me of flying temporarily, with the present commercial jets it could happen under certain circumstances and it did when we flew to Austin, Texas on a very hot day an updraft caught the right wing that made the landing on one wheel before setting down, it can happen.

Years ago when the Bell helicopters became useful I thought we all would be traveling in space above the ground. Mother Nature rules our destiny for air flights or on ocean waves – these problems will take more than a country boy's imagination to improvise. I was never in a submarine maybe it gets rough down there too. I always thought if I could fly it would be a so smoother ride no bumps like on the highways but up there sometimes you have to keep your seat belts fastened with the turbulence that suddenly comes up while flying through the fronts at such fast speeds.

You wonder what will be next if we can keep our heads straight, and taking "A Time to Live".

CHAPTER 39
Amateur Artist – Instructor

With this extended life, a few brushes, acrylic colored paints and a canvas and living alone I am enjoying seventy-five years later from the color book to a self-taught hobby of being an amateur artist.

Retirement changed a whole way of life for me. I always enjoyed seeing the beauty of nature while I was working full time every day of the week and thinking back to my youth age the transition in the movies was overwhelming to me. Seeing a colored movie the first time from the inevitable black and white on the screen it was the thrill of seeing the changeover to the gorgeous colors of "The Wizard of OZ" or a Disney cartoon movie of "Snow White and the Seven Dwarfs"." I would say I was about twelve years old 1937 whenever the theaters showed these would pinpoint the exact dates.

I drew the Disney "Seven Dwarfs" and colored them in a large scrapbook my folks bought me with my little allowance savings. This was the beginning but starting on the trumpet practicing I didn't have too much time for coloring. It also was more fun to be with my friends outside playing ball or so many things that kept me outside on the farm so I hadn't developed my interest in art.

I started a small painting class in our church basement and found with Nancy's influence it became a very enthusiastic substitute for the idleness the second week of retirement while being alone and school teaching kept my loving partner occupied. The classes started to increase each year and the demand became a great way to have others interested also to enjoy expressing their talents with a little guidance I had learned painting a few still life paintings. Having a group of people with such enthusiasm gave us a new way of life to live. I benefited being the instructor and as much as the old students did. I would paint the subject and make outline copies for the students to follow. I did this to save them time in the Monday morning classes each winter. They responded with overwhelming success and the happiness built up as the two month sessions were about to end. The first three you could sense the disappointment wanting to have a completed picture in a short time like the accomplished artist do on public television in a half hour.

We discovered the colors of nature, each shadow was a little darker not black like I thought at first. Anyway the other day I visited one of my friends and she had her class paintings framed and hung making the room so appealing and to think it was these classes spending many hours she did gave a personal daily look of her accomplishments using a brush, a canvas, different bottles of acrylic paints and plenty of patience knowing the time was well spent. After instructing over fifteen years there isn't a day that goes by that I think the time had been wasted.

I would like to finish with someone's thoughts, not mine, but can say when you see the master's work it opens a time to live, it's only a short time! I have experienced many young ones giving me their drawings and colorings. What more can there be to have the hearts of the innocents enter?

Art therapy is a form of expressive therapy that uses art materials, such as paints, chalk, glass and clay. The purpose of art therapy is much the same as in any other psychotherapeutic approach to maintain mental health and emotional well-being. Art therapists are trained to recognize the non-verbal symbols and metaphors that are communicated within the creative process; symbols and metaphors, which might be difficult to express in words. Art therapy is based on the belief that the creative process of art is both healing and life-enhancing.

Art therapists use the creative process and the issues that come up during art therapy to help their clients increase insight and judgment, cope better with stress, work through traumatic experiences, increase cognitive abilities, have better relationships with family and friends, and to just be able to enjoy the life affirming pleasures of the creative experience. By helping their clients to discover what underlying thoughts and feelings are being communicated in the artwork and what it means to them, it is hoped that people will not only gain insight and judgment, but perhaps develop a better understanding of themselves and the way they relate to the people around them.

Art making is seen as an opportunity to express one's self- imaginatively, authentically and spontaneously, an experience that, over time, can lead to personal fulfillment, emotional reparation and transformation. This view also holds that the creative process, in and of itself, can be a health-enhancing and growth experience.

- taken from *Art Therapy Can Aid Well-being,* author unknown

This I found helpful.

CHAPTER 40
The Postlude

You have read about how part of the prospected highlights from a farm boy growing through many experiences of happenings and duties that were performed being involved with the rural life in the Twentieth Century. The rural community is no longer left out, it has become an open door that magically transpired into the front seat we all are able to watch in our homes.

Watching the moon landing through a picture tube and recording on a tape showing a direct instant replay of an event that seemed impossible and the returning to earth at a precise spot in the ocean to recovering of the courageous men just unfolds an adventure we will see even more adventures in the Twenty First Century. When visiting with my family at the Smithsonian Institute at Washington, D.C. actually seeing the space capsule that touched down on the moon. This is not the fantasies of a science fiction author, it's real!

Away from the farm life experiences it's time to take advantage of seeing how others lived covering a share of our country and the world. One of the most exciting parts for me was seeing how the farmers worked and lived many in homes attached to the barns at the different locations on one of our short trips here on our earth. It was taking the family driving through the path on the back roads in Vermont with my seven passenger used station wagon. This one was called Smugglers Gap a little scary with the five children but luckily where we came out was near Stowe, Vermont.

The family wanted to see where the Maria Von Trapp lived. Julie Andrews starred in her story in "The Sound of Music" which we had seen recently. The whole family wanted me to drive in to where she lived but needing a cheap place for the seven of us to sleep I drove right by. The tears started flowing soon I knew I had to turn around and go back and drive in the driveway. The beautiful Chalet was covered with flowering window boxes. The timing was perfect, for in drove Mrs. Von Trapp with her convertible Corvair. We talked to her a few minutes while she showed us around and we saw where her husband was laid to rest in the back yard. It was on a hill Maria told us a similar setting where she lived in Austria. I took some quick 8-mm movies of her. My wife and kids never forgot this trip and neither did I.

Finally after the family left home to be on their own with a share of our retirement we had saved, Nancy and I with very short limited vacations in the past decided to explore the trips offered in some traveling catalogs and the prices were reasonable, we said let's give it a try. She booked a 21-day to Europe in May 1998, it turned out to be a real eye opener experience. Flying to London touring Windsor Castle and saw the changing of the guard at Buckingham Palace was a good start of being in different countries all but England spoke a foreign language, but very cordial that loved our dollars. Our guide was very informative throughout the trip.

From London we started by meeting all the bus passengers at the first overnight hotel and were together on the same bus and driver during the whole tour. Of the forty many were from different parts of the world all were friendly and could speak English. Riding to near the cliffs of Dover the bus and passengers were loaded into the Hovercraft with its four powerful Rolls-Royce engines to cross the English Channel to the port in Calais, France. I had my video camera checking the time programmed in. As we entered the Channel from the portage runway we approached the water crest, lifted somehow flying just enough above not to touch the water seeing the mist blowing, it was a fairly smooth ride. We zoomed to seventy miles an hour carrying many were business people living abroad reading their daily newspaper while crossing the thirty miles on open water. I had a good time asking some questions to the one next to me, they knew we were tourist. I timed it, took thirty minutes to the port landing. As a country farm boy what an experience this was, I guess I should say this whole trip also. The Hovercraft was soon to be history because it took about six hundred gallons of fuel in the loaded big air transport to go the thirty miles and with the fuel prices rising it no longer became a profitable trip. We were lucky because they terminated its expensive use about two years later. We were on the European main land as soon as the bus was unloaded on French soil the unfamiliar spectacular sites began. Our very friendly well informative guide from France was with us the whole trip pointing out were the German Bunkers still in place from World War II and other interesting facts as the tour proceeded in perfect shirtsleeve or sweater weather all having the best friendly time you could ask for.

As we traveled through to scenic Brussels, Belgium on to Germany to the immense mind boggling spectacular Cologne Cathedral, traveling by boat down the Rhine River seeing the ancient Castles. The Black Forests where our Coo-Coo clock was made, then up to the cold summit in the Alps, to Lucerne entertained by the Alpine yodeling and long sounding horns having a delicious meal in Switzerland passing the Swiss hillside farms over to Innsbruck, Austria that held the Winter Olympics. Visiting a small gorgeous cathedral where the choir was practicing for a wedding. The combination of music and art above was so enjoyable in such a short visit. Then busing across the countryside to Italy loaded on a sightseeing boat to the water streets of Venice and with a local guide visiting St. Marks impressive cathedral. We covered a good share of the open scenic farmlands seeing Nero's aqueducts of Italy, Isle of Capri, the uncovered volcanic ash streets with mosaic stone paintings still visible of Pompeii one was 2,000 year old "Beware of the Dog" in mosaic on a pedestal still very visible and museums that enhance your mind, we saw Michelangelo's 17' tall of David, his other marble statues and the breath taking Sistine Chapel paintings at the Vatican in Italy, In France the unfinished end of the 2,000-year-old Roman Empire stone road at Lyon, up in the Eiffel Tower, on to the Louvre seeing Di Vinci's, Mona Lisa, a statue of Venus, and Versailles near Paris in such a short time. When flying up thirty-five thousand feet watching the TV monitoring our position and sped back three thousand miles to good old USA.

Later in August 2001, seeing the twin towers in New York City one month before --- (9/11/2001)--- with the local senior group on a 10-day trip to Scotland. Further on a guided tour through Edinburgh Castle, then with the International talents coming out of Castle across the lift bridge with spectacular musical Tattoo performances into to an attach stadium, and then flying to the Emerald Green Isles of Ireland site seeing, up in the Blarney Castle ruins and kissing the fabled Blarney Stone. Coming back here to the USA with individual trips with each family, also trips with the Seniors Citizens around USA and Canada. Pretty well confined to our local community through the years in good health each trip was just wonderful, money was tight but fun and happiness was plenty.

WHAT ABOUT THE FUTURE?

Could it be better? Already I can see some experiences, larger farms, cloning plants and animals, living frozen embryo transfers to surrogate females or maybe a compact synthetic process, stem cells etc. leading to space travel---What is going to be like? No wires to the house everything maybe fuel cells; already satellite cell phones no wires. Energy made from abundant natural renewable resources maybe Hydrogen, Carbon Dioxide, Solar, Wind, Fusion, Enzymes or what can be replenished and grown efficiently for survival. It's all out there liked our visit to Nova Scotia seeing Alexander Graham Bell's Museum doing the impossible makes us thinks nothing is impossible.

I feel so fortunate to have been brought up on a farm with understanding, dedicated parents who had complete trust in me. They also gave what they could to our community, a thriving place at the end of the rainbow.

I tried to relay to you the simplicity of rural life and to tell you of the hardworking people and friendly animals that trusted us with a spiritual kindness we all enjoyed.

It is important we are mindful that the freedom we all enjoy today wasn't free without the unselfish dedication of the many generations who came before us. It was with their perseverance to invent, build, work, and protect with fierce patriotism that made America's Twentieth Century so remarkable. Their incredible gift has given us a purpose and a responsibility to continue on this path for generations to come.

Thank you for so many that have laid down their lives to make this wonderful freedom and Twentieth Century possible for the rest of us.

For it truly was ...

and will always be ...

A Time To Live

While on my way at last

It's been an adventure with all the years past.

I'm not going very far away

Just joining my friends I will be with someday.

- By C. Gordon Porter

Made in the USA
Charleston, SC
21 August 2013